seeking religion

The **Christian** Experience

J F Aylett and **Kevin O'Donnell**

Hodder & Stoughton
A MEMBER OF THE HODDER HEADLINE GROUP

Acknowledgements

The authors wish to thank the following for their generous help with this book: Canon Ian Dunlop; Miss Eva Pritchard; The Reverend David Bowers; Bishop Allison; The Reverend Huw Mosford; Peter Cotterell; Melvyn Fancy; the parents of Andrea Jackson; Marise, Mark, Rosalind and Sally; Sandy, Lynne and Alison; The Reverend Ros Parrett.

Minor adaptations have been made to some quotations to render them more accessible to the readership.

> *Notes*
> BCE stands for Before the Common Era.
> CE stands for the Common Era.
>
> The years are the same as BC and AD but this is a common way of dating that anyone can use.

Words in heavy print **like this** are explained in the glossary on page 63.

Order queries: please contact Bookpoint Ltd, 39 Milton Park, Abingdon, Oxon OX14 4TD. Telephone: (44) 01235 400414, Fax: (44) 01235 400454. Lines are open from 9.00–6.00, Monday to Saturday, with a 24 hour message answering service. Email address: orders@bookpoint.co.uk

British Library Cataloguing in Publication Data
A catalogue record for this title is available from The British Library

ISBN 0 340 74768 4

First published 2000
Impression number   10 9 8 7 6 5 4 3 2 1
Year   2004 2003 2002 2001 2000

Copyright © 2000 J F Aylett and Kevin O'Donnell

Cover photo from Christine Osborne Pictures/MEP.
Artwork by Daedalus Studio.
Typeset by Wearset, Boldon, Tyne and Wear.
Printed for Hodder & Stoughton Educational, a division of Hodder Headline Plc, 338 Euston Road, London NW1 3BH by Printer Trento, Italy.

The Publishers would like to thank the following for permission to reproduce copyright photographs in this book:
AKG, London: pp5, 6, 16, 48r; Mark Azavedo: p56r; Bureau Medicale de Notre Dame de Lourdes: p53; Christian Aid: p62l (Adrian Arbib), 62r (Leah Gordon); CIRCA Photo Library: pp14 (Martin Palmer) 20, 35b (Bipin J Mistry), 46l (John Fryer), 60; Corbis: pp41, 56l, 57; Philip Emmett: pp9br, 15, 21tr, 42, 47r, 52; Courtesy of Dawn French and Sue Hunter: p39; Melanie Friend/Format: p36; Sally Lancaster/Format: p61; Life File: pp34 (Emma Lee), 40 (Wayne Shakell), 43 (Sergei Verein), 51l (Mike Evans), 54 (Graham Burns); Network Photographers: p9tr; Christine Osborne/MEP: pp9l, 18 (G Bonatt), 21bl, 35t, 55; Hans Reinhard/OKAPIA/OSF: p17; Marcus Perkins: p27; David Rose: pp7, 10, 21tl, 22, 23, 46r, 47l, 48l, 49l, 50; Still Pictures/Bojan Brecelj: p19; Jan Thompson: p32b; Topham Picturepoint: p17; Alan Watson/Forest Light: p49r.

The Publishers would like to thank the following for permission to reproduce material in this volume:
The Archbishops' Council of the Church of England for The Apostles' Creed from *The Alternative Service Book 1980*, copyright © The Archbishops' Council of the Church of England and reproduced by permission; BBC TV for the extract from *England's Nazareth*; Christian Aid for the extract from *Christian Aid News*, April/June 1999; Peter Cotterell for the extract from *This is Christianity* (1985); Hugs illustration reprinted from *The Second Tiny Book of Hugs* by Kathleen Keating and Mimi Noland, published by HarperCollins Publishers. Copyright © 1988 by Kathleen Keating, drawings by Mimi Noland. All rights reserved. Reproduced by permission of Multimedia Product Development, Chicago, Illinois; Salvationist Publishing and Supplies Ltd for the extract from their publicity leaflet; The United Society for the Propagation of the Gospel for the extract from *USPG Network*; World Council of Churches for the Oikoumene logo.

Every effort has been made to contact the holders of copyright material but if any have been inadvertently overlooked, the publisher will be pleased to make the necessary alterations at the first opportunity.

Contents

The Christian religion began with a Jewish man called Jesus. He lived in the first century CE (Common Era) in Palestine (now called Israel). He travelled around the country, preaching and healing the sick. His followers believed that God lived in him more than anyone else.

His views caused trouble with Jewish leaders; they asked the Romans who controlled their country to execute him. The Roman **Governor**, Pontius Pilate, sentenced him to be crucified. This was a Roman punishment which meant the criminal was nailed to a cross. It was around the year 29 CE that Jesus was crucified in Jerusalem.

But Christians believe that God brought Jesus back to life; a number of people claimed that they had seen him alive after his death. Afterwards, they said, he went back up to heaven.

He had built up a group of followers; from these, he had chosen twelve to be his **apostles**. After his death, they risked their own lives to go on teaching his ideas. Within twenty years of his death, they broke away from the Jewish religion and started a new one – Christianity.

4

▲ This picture of the baby Jesus was painted by a Hindu artist in the seventeenth century

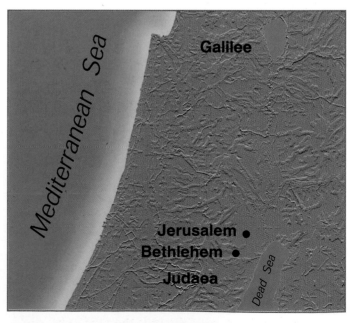

▲ Jesus was born in Bethlehem, in Judaea, and lived and worked in Galilee in the north. He was crucified outside the city of Jerusalem

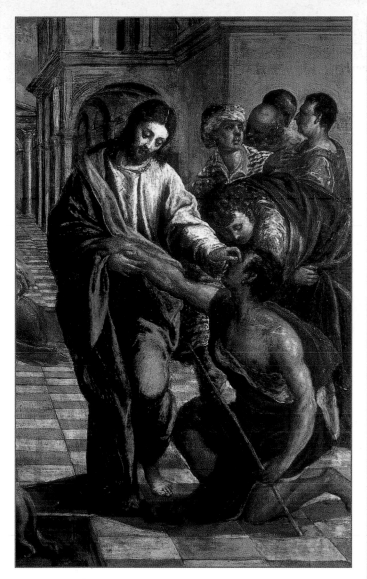

▲ *Jesus healing a blind man*

● **Jesus Heals a Paralysed Man**

A few days later Jesus went back to Capernaum, and the news spread that he was at home. So many people came together that there was no room left, not even out in front of the door. Jesus was preaching the message to them when four men arrived, carrying a paralysed man to Jesus. Because of the crowd, however, they could not get the man to him. So they made a hole in the roof right above the place where Jesus was. When they had made an opening, they let the man down, lying on his mat. Seeing how much faith they had, Jesus said to the paralysed man, 'My son, your sins are forgiven.'

Some teachers of the Law who were sitting there thought to themselves, 'How does he dare to talk like this? This is blasphemy! God is the only one who can forgive sins!'

At once Jesus knew what they were thinking, so he said to them, 'Why do you think such things? Is it easier to say to this paralysed man, "Your sins are forgiven", or to say, "Get up, pick up your mat, and walk"? I will prove to you, then, that the Son of Man has authority on Earth to forgive sins.' So he said to the paralysed man, 'I tell you, get up, pick up your mat, and go home!'

While they all watched, the man got up, picked up his mat, and hurried away. They were all completely amazed and praised God, saying, 'We have never seen anything like this!'

Mark 2: 1–12

5

Why was Jesus sent? His name and title might give some clues. 'Jesus' meant 'The Lord saves' or 'The Lord heals'. Saving and healing are about rescuing and mending something. Christians believe that Jesus came to heal the broken relationship between humans and God.

'Christ' was not his surname, but a title, meaning 'Anointed One'. Kings, priests and **prophets** were anointed with holy oil in the Bible. Christians believe that Jesus was anointed with the Holy Spirit, filled with God, because he had a special job to do. God had chosen him.

Christians see Jesus as a king, a priest and a prophet. As a king, Jesus was full of God's power. As a priest, Jesus would bring people back to God. As a prophet, Jesus would speak the word of God.

Jesus had an impact upon the people who met him. Read this story from the Gospels:

1 **a)** Write down four details about Jesus' life.
 b) Which one do you think a Christian would say was most important? Give reasons.
2 **a)** Look at the pictures on pages 4 and 5. Which of these words describe Jesus as shown in these pictures:
 kind; happy; proud; gentle; loving; strict; powerful; friendly; kingly?
 b) Which picture is most like your idea of Jesus? Explain how you decided.
3 **a)** What do (i) Jesus and (ii) Christ mean?
 b) Why are these names important for Christians?

▲ *Jesus ascends to heaven, with the disciples watching*

Jesus was called many other titles by the early Christians, such as Son of God. In the East, 'son of' meant that you were like someone. An insult might be 'you son of a camel'! To call someone a 'son of God' was to praise them – they were like God in some way. Jesus himself taught. *'Blessed are the peacemakers, they will be called sons of God.'* To call him *the* Son of God was to make him more Godlike, more full of God's love, than anyone else alive.

Another title was the Risen Lord. Christians believe that Jesus is not dead. He rose again. He is alive in a spiritual way. His tomb was found to be empty, and many of his followers claimed that they had had **visions** of him after his death.

Christians today still feel that Jesus has an impact upon them. A Catholic woman explains what Jesus means to her.

> ● He is a life-line, a friend and **counsellor**. Someone to talk to and air thoughts and feelings to – often a great help just to sort things out in my mind.
>
> I see Jesus as a figure of wisdom, goodness and kindness. If asked, he will help me see what I ought to do; through my **conscience**, he will let me know when I have done something I shouldn't have done.
>
> Jesus died on the cross to pay for the sins of the world. Every sin I commit causes him pain. You wouldn't deliberately cause pain to a friend so I wouldn't deliberately cause pain to Jesus.

1 a) Read what the Catholic woman says above. Why doesn't she want to hurt Jesus.

b) Think of a time when you have hurt someone. Why was this?

c) What did you do to try to make up with that person?

2 a) Many Christians would say that God doesn't find it difficult to communicate with humans: it is humans who find it hard to communicate with God. What do you think?

b) Christians think God communicated as clearly in the man Jesus. Do you think there could have been a better way?

3 a) Christians see Jesus as a king, priest and prophet. What do they mean?

b) Think of a time when you have felt really special, like a king, almost.

c) Think of a time when you have helped to put something right. A priest is a go-between, trying to bring peace and forgiveness.

d) Think of a time when you have had the courage to say or do what you know to be right. Prophets had to have great courage to speak God's word.

From small beginnings, the new Christian religion grew fast. In the fourth century CE, it became the official religion of the Roman Empire.

As Christianity spread to new lands, more people joined it. They brought their own ideas and customs to their new religion. So different ways of **worshipping** God developed.

In each country, Christian leaders were chosen. They did not always agree about how to worship God. The things they disagreed about were often trivial compared with all the things they did agree about. But these arguments led to splits within the Christian Church.

The first major split came in 1054 when Christians argued about who should lead the Church. Christians in eastern Europe and beyond were the Eastern **Orthodox** Church; its centre was in Constantinople (now known as Istanbul). Christians in the West became known as **Roman Catholics**. Their leader was the Bishop of Rome, now known as the Pope. He lives in Rome.

However, there were new arguments inside the Roman Catholic Church. In the 1500s, some followers protested at the way it was organised; they thought many Christians were not following what the Bible said closely enough.

So some of them set up new Churches. And, because they had been protesting, these new Churches were called Protestant. One of these was the Lutheran Church. The Church of England separated from Rome, but remained a mixture of the old and the new, in between Catholic and Protestant. Since then, many more different Christian groups have been formed.

Today, there are millions of Christians throughout the world, and about three hundred different groups, known as *denominations*. But we must remember that these are not different religions. They are like one big Christian family, with much in common. Above all, they all worship the same God.

▲ *Archbishop Gregorias, the Greek Orthodox Archbishop in Britain, blessing children*

7

1 Explain the meaning of each of these words:
(i) Christian; (ii) denomination;
(iii) Protestant.

◀ *The Christian family and some of its many branches*

Salvation Army 1865
Methodists 1764
Lutherans 1521
Plymouth Brethren 1827
Baptists
1540
Anglican Church 1521
Presbyterians 1612
Orthodox churches
Roman Catholic Church
1054

▼ *The logo of the World Council of Churches*

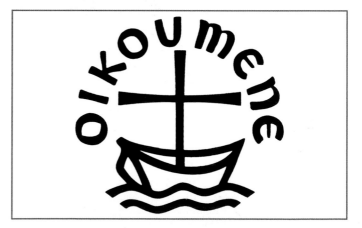

There are many different brands of washing powder for sale, but they are all basically the same thing. They all do basically the same thing. They may have different packaging, colours or names, but they all wash clothes.

There are many different brands or styles of Christianity, but they are all the same religion, believing the same things about God and Jesus – Methodist, Baptist, Roman Catholic, Anglican, Lutheran, Orthodox, Pentecostal, and so on.

The different Churches are now trying to work together much more, praying and worshipping together when they can in joint services. This movement to make peace between them is known as the **ecumenical** movement, from a Greek word meaning 'one world'. The symbol of the World Council of Churches is a cross in a boat, on the sea. This suggests that all Christians are 'in the same boat' in one world. They have more in common than they have that is different.

1 a) Write out the list of denominations in the order in which they were formed:
Anglican; Methodist; Baptist; Salvation Army; Roman Catholic; Lutheran.
b) Which of these Churches exist in your town? (Use Yellow Pages if you are not sure.)
c) In groups, write a letter to each Church, asking if someone could come to talk to you about their denomination. (It is polite to give plenty of warning.)
2 Draw the symbol of the World Council of Churches and write a sentence explaining what this means.

Imagine any family – there will be different personalities and interests. People will like different music, and might argue over what TV programmes to watch, or where to go for a holiday. Yet, 'blood is thicker than water' – they should have more in common than what separates them. Christian denominations are like this. People have different ways of worshipping the same God. Some like colourful symbols, some like traditional music, some like modern songs that they can clap and dance to. A church can feel very peaceful and special to a regular worshipper.

▲ Celebrating thanksgiving at a church in London

▲ An Armenian Orthodox Church service

▲ Modern worship with a church band

1 How do your tastes in music, clothes, hobbies and entertainment differ from those of your mother/father or another relative?

2 a) Look at the photographs of the three types of Church worship. What differences can you see?

b) If you ever attend religious worship, what type of worship do you prefer, and why?

3 Design your own badge for a united Christian Church. Then briefly explain your design.

The Christians' holy book is the Bible. But it is not really one book – it's lots of them, written by many different people at different times. It is more like a whole library in itself. In fact, the word *Bible* means *books*.

The oldest books of the Bible were written on long scrolls, made of clean, stretched animal skin. Later scrolls were made from the papyrus reed, an early form of paper. These were wound round rods and they had to be unrolled to be read out.

The first part of the Bible is the Old Testament. This contains Jewish **scriptures** from early times; it is holy to Jews, as well as to Christians. Much of it was written centuries before Jesus was born. So this part would have been learned by Jesus when he was young.

The New Testament comes after this and was written after Jesus died. His followers wrote about his life and teaching; four of these accounts are included in the Bible. We call them **Gospels**.

The New Testament also includes an account of the early days of the Christian Church; and letters written to guide these early Christians. For Roman Catholics, there is an extra part to the Old Testament. It is called the **Apocrypha**.

The Old Testament, or Hebrew Bible, was written over about one thousand five hundred years. This is made up of three main sections: the Law, the Prophets and the Writings – thirty-nine different books! These contain things like the Ten Commandments, the deeds of holy men such as Moses and King David, and poems of praise and wise sayings.

The New Testament contains five history books (four about Jesus, one about the early Christians), twenty-one letters, and a book of **prophecy**.

All of these books, at least sixty of them, are now printed in the form of one book, on thin paper. So much is crammed in between two covers! For Christians, the most important books in the Bible are the four Gospels, Matthew, Mark, Luke and John, which are about Jesus. ('Gospel' means 'good news'.)

▲ *A priest reads the Gospel. Note how decorative the book is. The Gospels are the most special part of the Bible for Christians*

1 a) How many books are in the Bible, and what are its two parts called?

b) Collect some different editions of the Bible together and see how these are laid out. Which are the easiest to follow? How many include the Apocrypha?

c) Write or speak to a minister or priest from a local Church and ask him or her to sum up what the Bible means to him or her in one sentence.

Christians see the Bible as a very special book. There are millions of books in the world, but the Bible tells people about God and how to live. It is like a Highway Code for living, a route map through life. Christians also believe that God can speak through the words of the Bible. They use Bible study notes to explain the text and to think about small sections each day.

▲ *We need maps to find our way. How do we find our way through life in general?*

Christians see the Bible as, in some sense, the word of God. They believe that the writers of the Bible were inspired, influenced by God. So, it is full of human words, through which God's message comes . . .

People sometimes say that they know something 'on good **authority**'. What they mean is that they have got the information from someone they trust. The Bible has this sort of authority for Christians because they trust God to tell them the truth. So they rely on the Bible.

Some Christians believe that every word of the Bible is true:

- The Bible is the word of God. He inspired the writers to tell us the truth. Of course, they chose how to tell us the truth. But they were all trying to do the same thing. They wanted to get across the truth of God.

  So I believe what the Bible tells me. God would not lie to me. When I read it, I know He is telling me the truth.

Others see it differently. The Bible contains the word of God, but it is also human, with various little mistakes. The main things that God wants us to know are true, but other things might be primitive ideas, or mistakes.

- They didn't have tape recorders in those days. It's only at a later stage that they thought, 'We must get this down.' They didn't have shorthand then. I don't think one can always say we've got the exact words of Jesus Christ. We've got what was remembered and there could have been small mistakes.

  People's beliefs were developing. Their accounts may have been affected by the beliefs which they'd developed. I don't think this reduces the Bible's authority.

One verse of the Bible declares, 'Your word is a lamp for my feet.' Stories and verses jump out at the reader and almost seem to speak to them, and meet their needs. There are striking, and different ideas in its pages which challenge people, such as:

- I am the way, the truth and the life. (Jesus)
- I am the Good Shepherd. (Jesus)
- The Lord is my shepherd, I shall not want. He makes me lie down in green pastures; He leads me beside still waters; He restores my soul. (King David)
- You have heard that it was said, 'You shall love your neighbour and hate your enemy.' But I say to you, love your enemies and pray for those who persecute you. (Jesus)
- God is love, and those who abide in love, abide in God, and God abides in them. (St John)

◀ Healing stories could be based on real events. The mind can affect how we feel

There are beautiful things in the Scriptures, but some things cause problems for some people. The first thing is the cruelty of some of the early stories in the Old Testament. People are put to death, and sometimes whole families and tribes are wiped out because they attacked the people of Israel. Joshua, for example, ordered that everyone in the city of Jericho should be killed. There are some nasty, horrific stories in the Bible. The worst story of all is about Jephthah's daughter. He had promised that he would sacrifice the first living thing that he saw if God helped the Israelites in a battle. It was his own daughter, and he had her put to death and offered on an altar to God!

These shocking tales are from a long time ago, when people were very savage and primitive. It is as though, the further on you get in the Bible, the more enlightened people become. Some Christians feel that God was slowly teaching his people the right way to live, and what he was really like. Primitive people could only learn a little at a time. By the time of Jesus, God was revealed as love, and people served him by forgiving and loving their enemies, not by slaughtering them!

A second difficulty that some people have with parts of the Bible is the many miracle stories. Did these really happen? Christians have different views on this, but all agree that if God is real, then unusual things can sometimes happen that science cannot explain. Clearly, people are cured, or feel much better as a result of prayer – whether this is the power of mind over matter or a supernatural power is questionable. People do feel that God's presence is with them, and they are guided by an inner feeling. There might well be forms of **extra-sensory knowledge** and powers as yet unknown to science.

1 Imagine that a person is afraid, unloved or confused about what to do. Which of the verses at the bottom of page 11 might help him or her? Say why.

2 **a)** Look up the Ten Commandments in Exodus 20: 3–17. Write a list of these in your own words.

b) Design your own Guide to Life, with a cover, and three sayings inside that make sense to you about how we should live.

Other Bible stories might be symbolic, and should not be taken at face value. For instance Adam and Eve might be fictional characters, but their story contains great truths about God and human beings. Myths and fables contain true morals even if the stories are made up.

▲ *Adam and Eve do not listen to what they know is right. They are tempted, and everything goes wrong. Human beings have a conscience, and a free choice in life between good and evil*

Other stories might be exaggerated, but based upon something real, such as Jesus feeding five thousand people with a few loaves and fish. Many think what really happened was that Jesus was prepared to share out what little food he had, and others had food with them, hidden away selfishly, and he shamed them into sharing what they had. The miracle was that Jesus stopped people from being selfish.

▲ *Jesus shared what little he had, maybe getting everyone else to share their food, too*

1 **a)** Read the story of one of the nasty events in the Bible from Judges 11: 29–40.
  b) Compare this with St Paul's hymn to love in 1 Corinthians 13. How is love described there?
  c) How do Christians explain how the Bible can contain such different passages as these?
2 Read the story of the feeding of the five thousand in John 6: 1–14. How do some people explain this? Does it make it any less of a miracle?

All Christians have the same basic beliefs. They sum up their beliefs in creeds. The word *creed* comes from a Latin word meaning *I believe*. So a creed is a kind of list of Christian beliefs.

There are various creeds. The one below goes back to the fourth century CE; at that time, it was said by adults who were being **baptised**. Today, it is often said as part of a church service.

> ● I believe in God, the Father **almighty**, creator of heaven and earth.
> I believe in Jesus Christ, his only son, our Lord.
> He was **conceived** by the power of the Holy Spirit and born of the Virgin Mary.
> He suffered under Pontius Pilate, was crucified, died and was buried.
> He descended to the dead.
> On the third day he rose again.
> He **ascended** into heaven, and is seated at the right hand of the Father.
> He will come again to judge the living and the dead.
> I believe in the Holy Spirit, the holy **catholic** Church, the communion of **saints**, the forgiveness of sins, the **resurrection** of the body, and the life everlasting. Amen.

The most basic belief is in God. Christians see him as their Father. Like a human father, he looks after them and protects them. But he is also powerful: he created the world; without God, there would be no world at all.

There is, for Christians, only one God. But they call him by three different names:
● God the Father
● God the Son (Jesus Christ)
● God the Holy Spirit
This idea is known as the Trinity. It means that three are united in the one God. But how can one God be three at the same time?

This is hard even for many Christians to understand fully. First, you should remember that Christians do not usually think of God as a person with a body. After all, a body has its limits; God has no limits at all.

Think of a cup of tea. Most of the tea we drink is blended. This means that it is made from more than one kind of tea. It might include teas from India, China and Sri Lanka. Each one of them adds something to the final taste. Each tea is different. But put them all together and what have you got? You have still got tea.

Or, think of water, steam and ice – all are H_2O. There are many ways in which many things can still be done.

▲ *One artist's idea of the Trinity. God the Father is symbolised as an old man, the Holy Spirit as a dove and the Son is Jesus, ascended on high. God is really invisible*

Christians do not usually make pictures of God, though they do of Jesus as he was a real man in history. This picture symbolises the Trinity, but God the Father and the Spirit are mysteries. They have no shape and cannot be seen. They are spiritual things, beyond our understanding. God is not really supposed to be an old man in the sky!

14

▲ *God is everywhere, all around us*

So God the Father, the Son and the Holy Spirit are all one. Together, they are God. But each one is also God. The Trinity helps Christians to understand God in different ways – and to see his greatness.

Perhaps it is easier to think of the Trinity as three parts of God. God the Father is God beyond us; God the Son is God with us, and God the Holy Spirit is God in us. God is everywhere, all around us.

God is a puzzle and a mystery to humans. God is transcendent – beyond us. God is symbolised by pure, blinding light, suggesting truth, life and something we cannot see properly. God is symbolised by a vast ocean. We can splash in the shallows, but it gets deeper and deeper. God is beyond our understanding. Yet, God is also symbolised by a caring father. This mysterious force is also love. All life comes from it and we are cherished by it.

Read these two stories and see what ideas they are suggesting about God:

> Two friends walked by the sea one day and saw a small child running to and from with a bucket, trying to fill a hole in the sand. The child said, 'I'm trying to put the whole sea into my hole!' The friends smiled and walked on. How are we like the little child when we think about God?

> A fish went around searching for the ocean. It travelled far and wide, looking here and there. It came to an older fish, and asked, 'Where is the thing called ocean?' 'It is all around you and within you!' answered the older fish.

1 a) What different ideas of God do you get from the words (i) almighty; (ii) Father?
   b) What ideas of God do symbols of light and an ocean suggest?
   c) What ideas of God are suggested by the story of the boy by the sea, and the fish looking for the ocean?
2 Write a few sentences saying what Christians mean by 'the Trinity'. Use ideas from pages 14 and 15.

▲ *Jesus Christ*

I believe in Jesus Christ, his only Son, our Lord . . .

The middle part of the creed is all about the Son, Jesus. It tells how he was born, how he died, and that he rose again. Eventually, he returned to the Father in heaven (this is known as the **Ascension**).

Christians also believe 'He will come again to judge the living and the dead'. The Gospels use vivid poetry to try to describe this time:

> ● When the Son of Man comes as King . . . he will sit on his royal throne, and the people of all the nations will be gathered before him. Then he will divide them into two groups, just as a shepherd separates the sheep from the goats. He will put the [good] people on his right and the others on his left.
>
> *Matthew 25: 31–3*

Christians have many different ways of making sense of this today, but all agree that Jesus has not yet finished with the world. It will not just fizzle out; evil will not go unpunished. It will end in the glory of God, and we will be judged by one who is Love. People will have to face up honestly to what they have done and who they are.

I believe in the forgiveness of sins . . .

All people make mistakes, and can do wrong, hurtful things to each other. Sin is hurting someone, yourself or God. God wishes to forgive, to make peace and to mend broken relationships. Forgiveness is not always easy and should never be cheap. It takes great courage, and can involve pain and suffering before things are put right. Jesus died on the cross, forgiving his enemies. Christians see the most perfect example of God's love in action, there, forgiving the whole human race for all their sins.

As one hymn states:

> There was no other good enough
> To pay the price of sin;
> He only could unlock the gate
> Of heaven and let us in.

I believe in the Holy Spirit . . .

The Holy Spirit is the part of God that lives on Earth, around us and within us. The Spirit is invisible, like the wind, but Christians say that they can feel the Spirit's effects. In the Bible, the Spirit is also symbolised by a dove for peace, fire for power, and water for life. Jesus once said, 'The water that I will give will become in them a spring of water gushing up to eternal life.' He was speaking about the Spirit.

▲ *'Living water' – a spring of fresh, bubbling water*

Many people say that they can sometimes feel a peaceful presence when they pray. The Bible calls the Spirit 'the Comforter'. Ian Dunlop, an **Anglican** priest, explains the comfort of the Holy Spirit like this:

● You can see it in a situation when somebody's very frightened. Somebody who is brave comes to sit beside them. And his bravery communicates itself to the frightened person. He can comfort people. 'The comforter' is another word for the Holy Spirit.

I have experienced that myself. I had a very painful accident when I was a soldier in the war. I broke my leg very badly and it was very painful. A person came and knelt beside me. It was actually a sergeant-major. Fancy a sergeant-major holding hands with you! But he did. He held my hand.

[People] were taking my boot off. That was the really painful moment. I could feel from the pressure of his hand in mine that my pain was becoming his pain. That strengthened me. It made it easier to bear. This is what the word 'comforter' means. It means to strengthen.

That's the nearest parallel I can give of what we mean when we say the 'god-strength' becomes our strength. This is how Jesus taught. He gave stories from real life. We should do the same. I couldn't say I understood the Holy Spirit if I'd not had those experiences to let me see it working at a human level.

1 **a)** If you had one magic wish to change the world, what would you wish for?
b) Design a CD cover to show what the world might be like when the Last Judgement has happened.
2 Which of the following do you think are sins? In each case, explain how you decided.
(i) Murdering someone; (ii) Being unkind to someone; (iii) Being cruel to an animal; (iv) An adult having a pint of beer; (v) Playing football on a Sunday; (vi) Eating unhealthy food and taking no exercise; (vii) Going to a party and enjoying yourself.
3 Draw a cross on a sheet of paper. Stick headlines from a newspaper around this, that are cruel and sinful events. At the bottom, write a sentence saying why Christians see the cross as proof of God's forgiveness.
4 **a)** What do Christians mean by the Holy Spirit?
b) Draw three symbols of the Spirit and say what they suggest.
c) Read what Ian Dunlop says about the Spirit. Describe a time when you needed comforting. Who helped you, and how?

▶ *The night turns to day. Can God bring light into the darkness of death?*

. . . and the life everlasting.

Christians believe that there is a life after death. They believe that you will meet your friends and family again. However, they do not expect life after death to be the same as life on Earth. It is a mystery and a surprise, operating by different rules from this world. It is beyond time and space, spiritual, not physical.

Christians do not really believe that heaven is up above us. The stars and planets are above us. Heaven is thought to be in another dimension, another level of reality, rather like the different levels in a computer game – when you are inside one, you have no way of knowing what it is like to be inside another.

> God himself will be with them:
> he will wipe every tear from their eyes.
> Death will be no more;
> mourning and crying and pain will be no more,
> for the first things have passed away.
>
> *Revelation 21: 3–4*

Christians hold funeral services to give thanks for the life of the dead person, and to commit their **souls** to God's care. It is a chance to gather family and friends and to grieve. It is right to be sad, and to shed tears, but Christian funerals also have a note of joy – death is not the end.

▲ *Time to move on to a different level*

◀ *A Christian funeral ritual in Jamaica. Mourners pray over the open coffin from the day of death to the burial day of the loved person*

In Britain, people tend to be reserved about showing emotion. This can be very different in other parts of the world. Afro-Caribbean funerals, for example, usually have an open coffin, and the mourners file past this to pay their last respects during the service – weeping, blowing a kiss, touching, sprinkling holy water. In ancient times, even great warriors wept openly and acted out their emotions – in the ancient Greek poems of Homer, for example, King Priam rolled in the dung and smeared this over him when he heard that his son was dead. Achilles knelt in the dust and wept when his good friend died. In the Bible, the custom is mentioned of mourners falling onto the ground and weeping (for example, Psalm 44: 23–36).

In modern Judaism, mourners rip their clothes to express grief. Letting out such feelings is important, and helps people to heal.

The Anglican prayer of Committal in the Funeral Service is as follows:

● Heavenly Father, by your mighty power you gave us new life, and in your love you have given us new life in Christ Jesus. We entrust N to your merciful keeping, in the faith of Jesus Christ your Son our Lord, who died and rose again to save us, and is now alive and reigns with you and the Holy Spirit in glory for ever.

19

1 a) Go around the class and each finish the sentence, 'Heaven is . . .'
  b) Where do Christians think heaven is?
2 Collect some **obituary** notices from a local paper. What phrases do people tend to use in obituaries and why?
3 When did you first become aware of death? Why do people feel uneasy talking about death?
4 How would you like to be remembered?
  a) What music would you like to be played at your funeral? Any special readings?
  b) What epitaph (inscription) would you like on a gravestone?
  c) Write your own obituary.
5 Read *Water Bugs & Dragonflies* by Doris Stickney (Mowbray). This tells a story to help young children understand about death and eternal life. In groups, write your own stories to read to young children on this subject.

▲ *An Anglican infant baptism service at a font*

Water ... Fresh, clean, powerful, strong, refreshing, life-giving! Water is a symbol of life, for all living things need water (most of our body is made up of water). Water symbolises other things, too. It suggests being made clean, forgiven. It also suggests death, for people can drown in strong currents and dangerous seas.

Baptism uses water, a universal, everyday symbol. Baptism is a ceremony where a person joins the Church. In many Churches this is done to an infant, as in the Roman Catholic, Anglican and Orthodox Churches. God is thanked for the child's new life, and it is welcomed into the Church. The ceremony involves pouring water over the child's head, or dipping the child into it three times, for the Father, Son and Holy Spirit. The water is in a large basin (a font) which is usually at the entrance of the Church. Baptism is the 'doorway' into the Church.

An infant cannot speak for him or herself, and so the parents and special friends – godparents – are asked to speak for him or her, making promises. They are expected to bring the child up in the Christian faith, and bring him or her to Church regularly. The child's name will be used in a public ceremony for the first time, and thus the first names are known as *Christian* names.

The water suggests being forgiven, washed clean, and given a spiritual new life.

Besides the water, other special actions might take place in a baptism service. The priest will pray over the child that any evil influence will be removed, and God's protection will come upon him or her.

▲ A baby is getting ready to be baptised. Here, the priest raises the Gospel over her head and prays for her to be free from evil

The sign of the cross will be made with blessed oil. The Orthodox call this **chrismation**, and the oil is known as chrism. It is a symbol of God's Spirit, soothing and healing like oil.

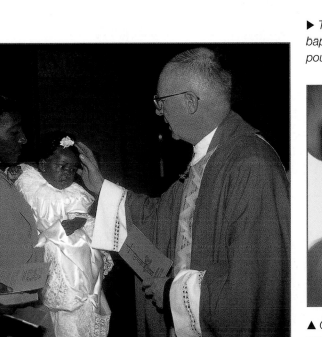

▲ The priest blesses the baby with oil during baptism

A lighted candle will be given. In the Anglican service, the priest says, 'Receive this light. This is to show that you have passed from darkness to light.' The light suggests God's presence.

▲ A lit candle given during the baptism service represents the light of Christ

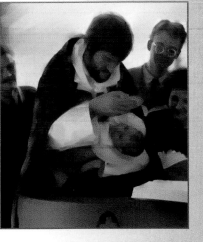

▶ The moment of baptism – the water is poured

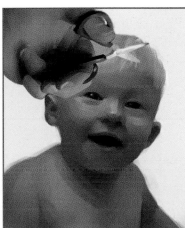

▲ Orthodox Christians dip the child into the font three times. As well as chrism oil and the candle, three pieces of hair are cut from the child's head to show that his or her life is dedicated to Christ

The Baptist Church does not baptise babies; a Baptist is usually at least twelve years old before baptism can take place. And he or she must ask for it to happen. Beforehand, Baptists are reminded that Jesus himself was thirty before he was baptised by John the Baptist. Below, a Baptist describes what happened at her baptism.

● You're baptised in front of everybody. It's your public witness that you want to follow Jesus. The usual way is for a minister to hold your back and your hand. Then, you go backwards into the water. Your feet actually come off the ground. My father, who baptises people, says the problem is getting you under the water because you float!

But the person who baptised me had had polio as a teenager. He hadn't got the strength in his arms to be able to baptise in that way. So I was baptised kneeling down and then I went forward under the water.

So there was no fear. I don't think I was as nervous as some people may be. I think that probably helped me to enjoy the feeling more.

I was baptised with four friends, which was nice. And you've got your family all round you, which is lovely. When your family are all Christians, you've got the support.

Afterwards, an elderly lady said to me, 'I expect you feel good now.' And I remember being a bit embarrassed and saying, 'I feel clean.' It sounded a silly thing to say. But I just felt totally clean – as if everything had been wiped out. That cleanness right inside was a splendid feeling.

▲ A believer's baptism in a Baptist Church

1 Brainstorm in groups about all the things that water can suggest.

2 Write about a time when you used water – to feel really clean, to quench your thirst or when you were in danger.

3 What three things does water symbolise in a baptism service?

4 Match up the following terms with their correct meanings:

font — holy oil used in baptisms
baptism — person responsible for a child's religious upbringing
godparent — basin holding water for baptism
chrism — ceremony where a person is received into the Church

5 What does oil symbolise in a baptism service? What is done with this?

6 Draw a candle and write around this all the things it might symbolise.

7 Why is a newly baptised person given a lighted candle?

8 a) In groups, discuss reasons for and against baptising infants. Be ready to share your reasons with the other groups.

b) What do you think the Baptist meant by saying, 'I felt totally clean'?

9 Design a baptism card, showing symbols of baptism on the front, and details of the baptism service inside. Have space for a photo of the child, names of godparents, date and place where the service took place, and who performed it.

Of course, a baby cannot make decisions about its future. That is why it has godparents to help with its upbringing. But the time comes when a young person must choose for themselves: do they wish to be a Christian or not?

Young members of the Church of England and the Roman Catholic Church usually make their decision at any time from about twelve years onwards. If they decide to become an adult member of the Church, they say so at a special service.

This service is called *confirmation*. The young person is *confirming* (or agreeing to) the promises which the godparent made for him or her years earlier.

During the service, a **bishop** will place his hands on the young person's head; or he may anoint them with oil; or he may simply hold their hand. But first he will ask some questions just to make sure that the person knows what they are confirming.

A Roman Catholic bishop lays his hands upon a young person to confirm them. Catholics can receive communion before they are confirmed; Anglicans usually do so after they are confirmed, but some parts of the Anglican Church are changing this rule so that younger children can take communion.

In the latest Anglican service, the bishop asks questions which demand a response:

● Do you **reject** the devil and all rebellion against God?

I reject them.

Do you **renounce** the deceit and corruption of evil?

I renounce them.

Do you **repent** of the sins that separate us from God and neighbour?

I repent of them.

Do you turn to Christ as Saviour?

I turn to Christ as Saviour.

Do you submit to Christ as Lord?

I submit to Christ.

Do you come to Christ, the way, the truth and the life?

I come to Christ.

The candidate then recites the Apostles' creed in three parts, prompted by three questions from the bishop:

● Do you believe and trust in God the Father?

Do you believe and trust in his Son Jesus Christ?

Do you believe and trust in the Holy Spirit?

▲ *A Roman Catholic bishop confirms a girl*

Of course, this ceremony is very important. The young person must believe the answers he or she makes. He or she must also know enough about Christian beliefs to understand what he or she is saying.

▲ *The actual moment of confirmation is when the bishop lays his hands upon the candidate*

The laying on of hands is a way of giving a blessing in the Bible, and God's Holy Spirit can be transmitted through a person's hands. The touch of the hands suggests that the candidate is accepted, wanted, welcomed by the bishop, the Church and God. Caring, gentle touches are very important for humans – they express love. It is no different in religion. The bishop also sees himself as a successor to the first apostles, appointed by Jesus. It is as though their hands are reaching out to the candidate through the bishop, and the hands of Jesus are behind these.

▲ *A hug keeps back the shadows*

Hugs and touches of the right sort make us feel safe, loved and happy. As one person has said, 'The wonder is: when we seek to transfer our energy in a hug, our own strength increases!' To Christians, confirmation is a little touch from God.

An Anglican prayer for the newly confirmed:

> Defend, O Lord, these your servants with your heavenly grace,
> that they may continue yours for ever,
> and daily increase in your Holy Spirit more and more until they come to your everlasting kingdom. Amen.

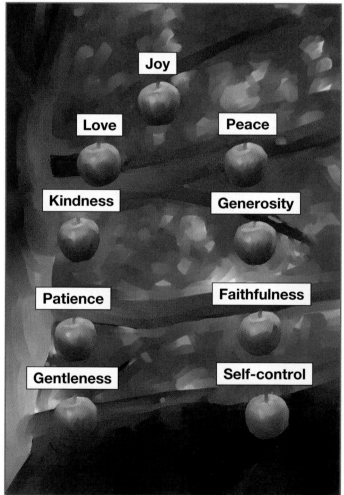

▲ *The fruits of the Spirit*

Christians believe that the presence of God's spirit within a person helps to change them for the better, slowly but surely. St Paul writes about the nine fruits of the Spirit in Galatians 5: 22–23. These are the qualities that should be growing in a person who claims to be Christ's.

Ian Dunlop is a **canon** at Salisbury Cathedral. This passage is based on notes he gives pupils in confirmation classes. In this extract, he writes about sin.

- Imagine that you are a man from Mars who has arrived on Earth. But you cannot pick up the wavelengths of this world, so you are totally deaf. You discover a piano. You would be able to discover everything about the piano, except what it is *for*.

You cannot understand it because you cannot grasp its purpose. Now, if someone could open your ears and play the piano to you, then *and only then* could you *understand* the piano.

Can you imagine a piano coming into existence if it had not first been thought of in the mind of a musician? Can anything have a purpose if it was not first conceived in a mind?

Now, your own life cannot be understood unless it has a purpose. It cannot have a purpose if it was not conceived in a mind. That mind we call God.

If God has a purpose for you, anything you do which helps to achieve that purpose is *good*. Anything that falls short of it is *sin*. The Greek word for 'sin' means 'to miss the mark'. We therefore need to know what the mark is.

Suppose a car stopped by you and the driver asked, 'Am I on the right road?' What question do you *have* to ask him?

1 Copy out and complete this paragraph: Young people confirm their beliefs at a service called _____. They agree to the _____ made by their _____ when they were babies. In the Church of _____ this happens from the age of _____.

2 **a)** In groups, read carefully the six questions asked at an Anglican service. In your own words, write down what you think any two of these questions mean.
b) Decide as a class which one you find most difficult to understand.
c) In groups, work out what it means.

3 **a)** Talk about a time when you have been sad and a caring touch or hug has helped you.

b) Draw around your hands and write in these what the bishop's hands stand for in the confirmation service.

4 **a)** Read Canon Dunlop's notes. What question would you ask the driver?
b) This is another of Canon Dunlop's questions. What does the word 'good' mean in these phrases: (i) a good game; (ii) a good medicine; (iii) a good rifle; (iv) a good instrument of torture?
c) In groups, decide what you mean by a 'good person'.
d) Compare your answers to (c). Are they very similar or not?

Having a strong faith has its advantages and disadvantages for a teenager. The last chapter was about making confirmation promises. It is not always easy to stick to them. Religion, for many people, is their private business. Others are very happy to discuss their feelings and encourage others to believe. Here are two situations that might be awkward for a Christian teenager.

▲ *Not one of the 'in-crowd'. Left out because of beliefs*

26

Some people always mock what they do not understand. If a person has a strong faith, someone is bound to try to make fun of it, shouting 'Alleluia!' at him or her, or calling him or her a 'Holy Joe'. This can hurt, and make a person want to keep his or her feelings very private.

You might have met someone you really like who wants to go out with you, but you know he or she has no time for your religion, and he or she will try to persuade you to give it up. You are young, and want to have fun, but you want to be true to your beliefs, too.

Having a faith can be a joy and a strength, though, too. These teenagers explain what being Christian means to them.

Marise (aged 19)
- At first [my workmates] were astonished I was in the Salvation Army because I looked too modern! But now they respect my beliefs. Sometimes people ask for my opinion *because* I'm a Christian. That way I get a chance to be a witness for Jesus.

Mark (aged 16)
- Christians can feel at peace with anyone, loving and forgiving them, if it's necessary. It is not easy but it is a better way of living than if you're not Christian.

Rosalind (aged 13)
- It helps me to feel that someone is always there to help me when I need it. It is important to me because Christianity is what I believe in, and no other faith.

Sally (aged 16)
- I can talk to God whenever I like and I know he is listening.

Christian teenagers can get bored in Church for the services might be old or too quiet. They want to worship in their own way, with lots of energy, movement and imagination. They want to have other young Christians around them to praise with. There are many styles of alternative youth worship. Some can be Rave style, with ambient music, dancing, religious pictures, incense and candles.

Some teenagers prefer worship led by a modern band, where they can clap and raise their hands.

Others prefer times of quiet and silence with simple chants and flickering candlelight, where they can sit, kneel or lie on the floor.

Many Church youth groups go away to special young people's events such as the Greenbelt Arts Festival. Here, there are modern bands of all styles – heavy rock, folk, Club style, imaginative worship times, talks and Bible studies, and lots of fun times, with clowns juggling or places to relax with ambient music where young people can sit and chat, all through the night!

◄ *Express yourself! A modern worship service gives people freedom to move around as they wish*

1 Read what the teenagers say on page 26.

a) Why were Marise's workmates surprised she was in the Salvation Army?

b) What does that tell you about people's attitudes towards Christians?

c) Take any one of the other statements. Explain why that teenager feels being Christian is important to them.

d) Which reason do you think is best? Give *your* reasons!

2 **a)** What problems does the person have in the illustration on page 26?

b) Why do people make fun of things they do not understand?

c) What sort of things would put you off someone with a strong faith, and what might attract you to them?

d) What problems does the person with the girlfriend or boyfriend on page 26 have? What would you do in that situation? Is the friend worth bothering with if he or she will not respect your opinions?

3 List the styles of modern worship that some Christian teenagers enjoy. Which do you prefer, and why?

4 Imagine that you were designing a programme for the Greenbelt Festival. What sort of events would you include?

Christians do not have any special religious acts which they have to perform at home. But Jesus asked his followers to pray to God. So, many Christians believe you need to pray privately every day to lead a Christian life.

Jesus said,

> ● But whenever you pray, go into your room and shut the door and pray to your Father who is in secret; and your Father who sees in secret will reward you.
>
> *Matthew 6: 6*

Many Christians worship alone, or with their family. Prayers can be said anywhere – standing, walking around, sitting, lying down or kneeling. There are no rules. Some people prefer to kneel, as this is showing **humility**. Some cross themselves, reminding themselves that Jesus died for them. Orthodox Christians have an **icon** corner. They face the icons – holy pictures of Christ or the Saints – when they pray. Some Catholics have a shrine in a corner, with candles, a **crucifix** and a statue of Jesus, Mary or one of the Saints. This helps them to concentrate. Christians might make up their own prayers, or use traditional ones that they have been taught. Christians may also say grace before and after a meal. It is a way of thanking God for their food.

▲ *Thinking, confessing, asking for help . . . prayers can involve all these things*

Prayer can often be about being still and quiet, just feeling peaceful and listening. As a Psalm says,

> ● Be still and know that I am God.
>
> *Psalm 46: 10*

Five other things can be included as well:

1 Praise

● Christians believe that God has created the world and everything in it. So they want to praise God. It means telling him how great and good he is.

2 Thanking

● They often want to thank God for the gifts he has given the world. Or perhaps, they thank him for a gift he has given them.

3 Asking forgiveness

● If Christians feel they have acted wrongly, they may think they have sinned. So they ask God to forgive them.

4 Asking for yourself

● Perhaps they have been sick and want to ask God's help to get better. Or, if they have done wrong, they would ask him to give them the determination not to do it again.

5 Asking for others

● Someone may be ill in the family and the prayer is asking God to make them better. Sometimes, the prayer might be asking for something everyone wants, such as world peace.

1 a) Draw your own chart showing the five parts of prayer.

b) Praise, thanking, asking forgiveness, asking for yourself or someone else – write a sentence about a time when you have felt the need to do this in everyday life (not just in prayers).

Does prayer work? What does it do? Here are some different ideas. See what you think of these.

It helps to think someone is listening, and to talk your problems out!

Being quiet and asking for help often gives you the right idea, or the courage, to answer your prayers!

Maybe there are all kinds of connections between our minds, other people and the world that we do not understand yet. Thinking good things about others might allow good things to happen to them.

Prayer opens people up to God's power. We don't understand how it works, but it makes all sorts of things happen. It is different from wishing for things!

▲ Different ideas about the value of prayer

Christians say that prayer is not like magic, or a slot machine. You cannot make things happen. You seek God's guidance and help. It might be better that some things you pray for do not happen to you. Sometimes, prayers seem to be answered, and sometimes they seem to go unanswered. Some people are cured, amazingly, some are not. Many who ask for prayer when they are sick say that it helps them and makes them feel more at peace, even if they are not cured. Perhaps prayer opens up all sorts of possibilities. An answer to a prayer might feel like a coincidence, but a believer once said, 'When I stop praying, the coincidences stop happening!'

Jesus once taught his disciples to pray, and gave them the Lord's Prayer:

Our Father in heaven,
hallowed be your name,
your kingdom come,
your will be done,
on earth as in heaven.
Give us today our daily bread.
Forgive us our sins
as we forgive those who sin against us.
Lead us not into temptation
but deliver us from evil.
For the kingdom, the power, and the glory are yours
now and for ever. Amen.

Still yourself:
Sit comfortably in a quiet place.
Breathe deeply and slowly for a few minutes.
Imagine a peaceful scene.
Repeat a phrase over and over again, in your mind,
such as 'May I be at peace ...'
Count ten breaths and then open your eyes when
you are ready to finish.

This is a simple meditation, but it could be turned into a Christian prayer by repeating Jesus' name, or a verse from the Bible. When people are quiet and still inside, they are able to pray better.

Some people like to do something when they pray, such as lighting a candle. Orthodox, Catholic and some Anglican Churches have candle stands. The lit candle represents prayers being offered up to God. The light suggests life and hope. Lighting candles has become more and more popular in modern society – witness the scenes when Princess Diana died. People offered flowers and lit candles.

▲ Lighting up . . . offering a lit candle as a prayer

Some people like to move their bodies as they pray. People feel much freer about praying in their own way.

Bowing or kneeling suggests humility; open hands or raised arms suggests surrender, and being open to God. Crossing yourself reminds Christians that Jesus died for them; hugging yourself and rocking feels safe and secure, being bathed in God's love.

▲ Bodily movements in prayer

1 Read through the Lord's Prayer. How many of the five aspects can you find in this?
2 Design a quiet place where you would like to reflect and to be still. Where would this be and what would be in it? How might you use light, water, decorations and music?
3 In groups, read through the ideas of what prayer actually does for people. Which do you agree with? Which are the most helpful? Can you add any others?
4 Try the meditation exercise on page 29. How did it feel? What helps you to be quiet? Are there special times, special places, special things which help you?
5 Can you describe a special occasion when you remember being quiet, for example when you heard some sad news?
6 a) Why do some people light a candle when they pray?
   b) Can you think of a time when you needed to do something to express how you felt (like putting flowers on a grave)?
7 Look at the movements that can be used in prayer. Suggest suitable movements for each of the five aspects of prayer. (You can think up some of your own.)

30

◀ *The sign of the fish – a symbol for Christ*

In the years after Jesus died, public services were out of the question. Christians were wanted people. If they were caught, they were put to death. So Christians met secretly to worship God. Many of these services happened in people's homes; others took place in the **catacombs** or similar hiding places.

The word 'church' means 'assembly'; Christian gatherings were known as 'churches' and still are. They did not actually *build* churches until they felt safe. The first Roman Church was started in 313 CE. Even so, for long afterwards, there were not enough buildings. So services were often held in the open air.

The early Christians had special signs to recognise each other, such as the Ichthus, or fish sign.

The word 'icthus' meant 'fish' in Greek. (Don't forget that most of the first Christians spoke Greek.) Jesus talked about making people 'fishers of men', but the letters of 'icthus' each stood for something – Jesus Christ, Son of God, Saviour – in Greek.

Another early symbol was the 'Chi-Rho' which formed a design from the first two letters of 'Christ' in Greek.

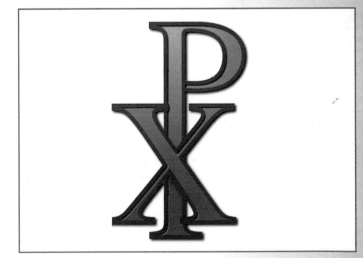

▲ *The Chi-Rho symbol*

1 Using the English words 'Jesus' or 'Christ', work out a secret symbol that Christians could use to recognise one another.

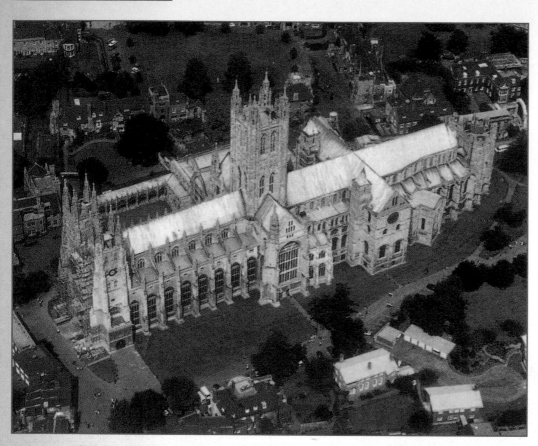

▲ *A view of Canterbury Cathedral from the air. This is the seat of the Archbishop of Canterbury. Notice the building's shape, designed as a cross*

Special, large churches where the bishop has his seat are known as cathedrals. Canterbury Cathedral is the seat of the Archbishop of Canterbury. Other churches can be any size. A chapel is a small church attached to another building, such as a school or a hospital. Protestant church buildings are often called chapels.

Different Christian groups have different designs for their buildings.

The Society of Friends (Quakers) calls its buildings Meeting Houses. There is no altar or pulpit, so people sit facing each other.

Anglican or Roman Catholic Churches have an altar as the main item, where communion is celebrated. These can be highly decorated, with candles, a cross and flowers.

A Methodist or Baptist Church will usually have a raised pulpit, and a table. The reading of Scripture and the preaching are seen as the most important item in the service. Communion is celebrated on the holy table, which is plain and simple.

▲ *A Baptist pulpit and table*

Inside an Anglican church.

Look for:

- *the font*
- *the altar, with a crucifix*
- *stalls where the choir sits*
- *hassocks (cushions) to kneel on*
- *pews where people sit*
- *the pulpit for **sermons***
- *the lectern for the Bible*
- *the hymn board*

1 Copy out and complete this grid, using the clues below.

 a) One denomination which meets in chapels.

 b) These singers have special seats.

 c) What the congregation sit in.

 d) This is a small church attached to another building.

 e) Look for it on the altar.

 f) Main feature of many chapels.

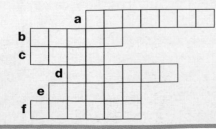

2 Look at the drawing above and the list of items that are found in an Anglican church. Write the numbers 1–9 on separate lines, and write the names of each item in the correct order.

3 If you had to hold a service in the open air, what would you use for (i) an altar and (ii) a pulpit? Give reasons for your choices.

4 a) Do you have a special place – perhaps quiet and secret, or a place you have been to on holiday?

 b) Design a modern Christian place of worship. What shape would the building be? What type of decoration would you use? What about music and seating? Use your imagination – this is *your* idea.

◀ *A time to share and enjoy*

Eating together is a time of fun and sharing. Everyone has to eat, rich or poor, the Queen or a tramp. When people eat together, they are all on the same level. A special meal that you can remember might be a huge and expensive party. It does not have to be. Sometimes, the simplest food, shared out, can be extra special. One person remembers sharing out a pack of dried bananas:

> ● We had been climbing in the Lake District, and we were very tired. We still had a long way to go, and everyone had finished their lunch ages ago. Then, someone pulled a pack of dried bananas out of their rucksack. They looked disgusting – all squashy, brown and wrinkly. But we didn't care, they were sweet and tasted good! We all gathered round and broke off bits and pieces so everyone had some. It gave us the energy, a lift, to keep going!

The last meal which Jesus ate with his disciples was at the Jewish feast of Passover. He broke some bread and shared it round, saying, 'Take, eat, this is my body.' Afterwards, he passed them a cup of wine. This time, he said, 'It is my blood which is shed for you. Do this in memory of me.'

Most Christians still share bread and wine, just as Jesus told them to do. It happens as part of a special service. Christians use several different names for this service.

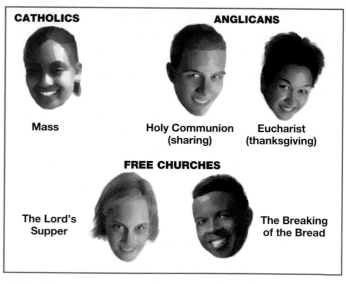

▲ *The different Christian names for bread and wine*

The Quakers do not have holy communion as they feel every meal is special. The Salvation Army do not have any ordained ministers, and they stress that we can feel the presence of Jesus in many ways without the bread and wine.

> 1 a) In pairs, think of a special meal you have shared.
> b) Why did the hill climbers find the meal of dried bananas so special?

◀ A Coptic communion service. Notice the flat, Eastern style bread

Roman Catholics and Anglicans come forward to the altar rail, and the priest gives them the bread and wine. The bread is often unleavened – made without yeast – so it is flat and crisp, easily digested.

Orthodox priests come out to the people, and give them the bread and wine on a spoon, mixed together. The bread is leavened and in small chunks.

Free Churches usually have non-alcoholic wine in small glasses. The bread is leavened, and cut into chunks. These are passed around.

Methodists have leavened bread and small glasses of wine, but they come forward to receive these from the minister.

The service, too, varies. But it reminds all Christians of how Jesus died for them. It brings them especially close to God. Orthodox Christians often do not eat meat for days beforehand.

Many Christian churches hold a service like this every Sunday. They may also hold a Family Service; young people are encouraged to come to these services and to join in worship.

Most services are made up of many parts. The picture of a church on page 33 gave you all sorts of clues about what may happen during a service.

It may include:
- prayers
- singing of hymns and psalms
- reading from the Bible
- a sermon by the priest or minister (probably explaining something from the Bible)

However, the aim is always the same: a group of Christians is gathering together to worship God. They offer him their praise; they confess their sins; and they hope for guidance to live better in the future.

▶ An Orthodox girl receives communion on a spoon

Christians have different ways of worshipping the same God. Some services are longer or shorter, some traditional or very modern.

The Reverend Huw Mosford returned to Wales from Jamaica. He says the Church in Britain has a lot to learn from Anglicans in the West Indies.

> ● Worship here is very **staid**, we need more freedom. We should show love in our services and not just go to sit in our seats for one hour precisely. In Jamaica you put your watch behind you when you go to church. That was something I had to learn.
>
> They taught us to take time over worship and to sing more. Worship and church life is so important to Jamaicans. They all *belong* to a church. It is very important in their lives.
>
> *Network* magazine

▲ *At this Methodist service in America, the congregation clap and dance to the music. This is just one way of worshipping*

Some Christians use modern instruments and short, catchy tunes. They might clap or dance along.

Orthodox Christians have many things to look at and to do in their buildings. They reverence an icon when they enter by bowing low and kissing it. This shows their love and respect for what it represents. They can also light candles.

A Friday service at the African Israel Church in Kenya.

> ● The people came singing, beating drums and dancing. When they reached the church, they all shouted 'Halleluya' and then entered. They continued singing, jumping and making a lot of noise. When one of the church elders stood up, the singing stopped.
>
> But the church was still noisy because some, who had received the Holy Spirit, went on praying and jumping about. Then there was a prayer which lasted ten minutes. A man preached; and then eight women stood and confessed their sins.
>
> When they were saying the final prayer, a woman fell on the ground. She, too, had received the Holy Spirit. When prayers are being said, all the windows and doors are shut. People then gave offerings as they left the church. Some went home; and the rest walked along the road, singing and praising the Lord.
>
> F B Welbourn and B A Ogot:
> *A Place to Feel at Home*

1 **a)** List the different names for holy communion and explain their meaning. Try to find out where the name 'mass' comes from.

b) Look at the photographs and text on page 35. Describe any two methods of receiving communion that different Christians have. What do these different methods suggest?

c) Look up the words of Jesus in Mark 14: 22–24. What does he say the bread and wine represent?

2 Look back at the picture on page 33. Write down this list of events in a service: (i) sermon; (ii) singing hymns; (iii) prayers; (iv) reading from the Bible. Beside each, write down which part of the church is most linked with it.

3 Design a service leaflet for a Church service, using the information on page 35. Make up some prayers and instructions. Illustrate this with at least one picture. The service can be either traditional or modern. If modern, what sort of songs might you have, and what movements might people be invited to make? Would they do anything else, like lighting a candle?

4 **a)** Read this page. What does the Reverend Mosford think is good about West Indian services?

b) How is the service in the African church similar to those in the West Indies?

One of the key people in most Christian communities is the person who leads the congregation in worshipping God. The Christian Churches have different names for this person. Baptists use the word 'pastor'; it means shepherd. Methodists call him or her a 'minister'; it means someone who serves others.

Many Churches have 'priests'. Some priests today are women, though women priests are not allowed in the Orthodox or Roman Catholic Churches. Many Anglican Churches do accept them. Anglicans have priests, though they also call the priest in charge of a parish 'vicar' or 'rector'. The vicar's assistant priest is called a curate.

Of course, these people have to be trained. It may take up to four years or more. At the end, there is a ceremony when the priest is **ordained**. A bishop lays his hands on the priest's head. It is a sign that God will help the priest in his or her work.

So what is their work? The pictures on page 38 will give you some idea of what it is like.

As you will see, being a priest is not just a job. It is a way of life.

Protestant ministers, Anglican and some Orthodox priests are allowed to marry. Roman Catholic priests are not normally allowed to marry, as it is felt that a single man can give more time to the parish.

Miss Eva Pritchard is a **lay** minister. She works as a **chaplain** in a Liverpool hospital.

● It's amazing how quickly you find you can't learn prayers in advance. They must come from the situation. I had no control over them. The words came directly from the Holy Spirit.

You'd be surprised, but sometimes God doesn't want me to go. Sometimes, I can't get through to the sick person. It has to be someone else. But, if God does want to use me, he will. When people are ill, they usually just want God – or Jesus.

I was called to one woman who was critically ill. The young nurse said, 'It's no good going in. She's in a coma.' I said, 'But I can pray, can't I?' She said, 'It's no good. She won't hear you.'

But I knew that if God wanted me to help, he'd show me what to do. God took over. I lay my hands on her head and the prayers just came. Suddenly, the woman sat bolt upright, and looked me straight in the face. 'Thank you, my dear,' she said. 'That was the most lovely prayer.'

chasuble

stole

alb

▲ *A priest in eucharistic robes (vestments) and in choir dress. Choir dress is worn to take Morning or Evening Prayer when communion is not being shared. These robes go back to ancient traditions. Some go back to Roman times, and the days of the first Christians*

1 a) Draw the priests opposite.
   b) Why do you think they wear special clothes like these?
   c) Write down the advantages for priests of being married.
   d) Write down any disadvantages.
2 a) Read about Miss Pritchard's work. How do you think her visits help the patients?
   b) How does she decide what to say to them?
   c) If you were in hospital, do you think you would like to be visited by a hospital chaplain? Explain your answer.

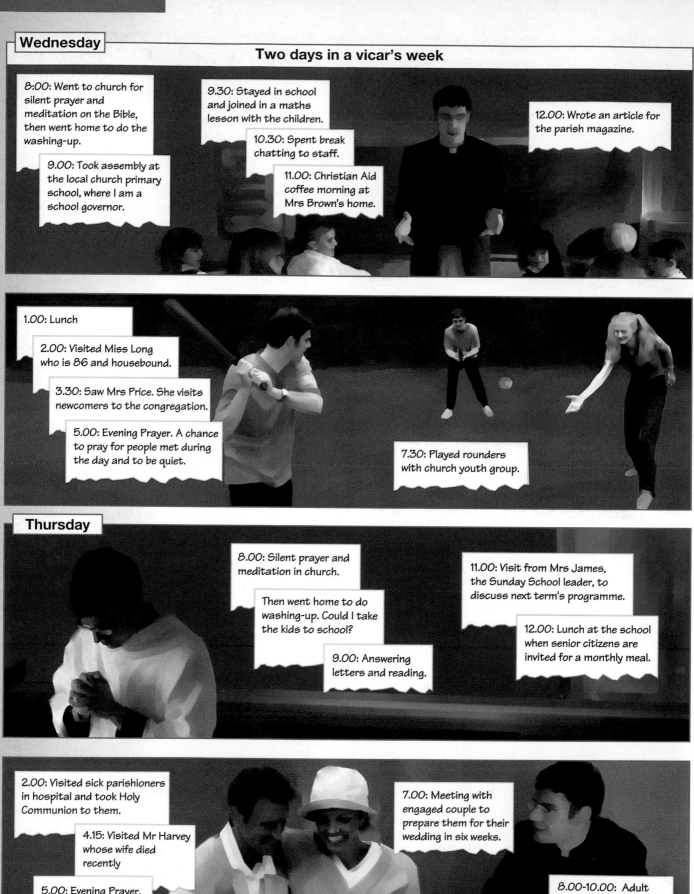

Wednesday

Two days in a vicar's week

8:00: Went to church for silent prayer and meditation on the Bible, then went home to do the washing-up.

9.00: Took assembly at the local church primary school, where I am a school governor.

9.30: Stayed in school and joined in a maths lesson with the children.

10.30: Spent break chatting to staff.

11.00: Christian Aid coffee morning at Mrs Brown's home.

12.00: Wrote an article for the parish magazine.

1.00: Lunch

2.00: Visited Miss Long who is 86 and housebound.

3.30: Saw Mrs Price. She visits newcomers to the congregation.

5.00: Evening Prayer. A chance to pray for people met during the day and to be quiet.

7.30: Played rounders with church youth group.

Thursday

8.00: Silent prayer and meditation in church.

Then went home to do washing-up. Could I take the kids to school?

9.00: Answering letters and reading.

11.00: Visit from Mrs James, the Sunday School leader, to discuss next term's programme.

12.00: Lunch at the school when senior citizens are invited for a monthly meal.

2.00: Visited sick parishioners in hospital and took Holy Communion to them.

4.15: Visited Mr Harvey whose wife died recently

5.00: Evening Prayer. Time for prayer and quiet. Then went home to be with the family.

7.00: Meeting with engaged couple to prepare them for their wedding in six weeks.

8.00-10.00: Adult Bible Study Group. Discussions about the meaning of the Letter to the Ephesians.

38

● Ordained Women?

Various Churches have allowed women to be ordained in recent years. It used to be thought that this was not the right role for a woman. There were many reasons:

- Men should be in charge in Church and in society. Women should be more involved with their families.
- Women were too emotional, and men were more rational. Women could not be trusted to lead a parish.
- Women were weaker than men, and were not up to the job, physically.
- Ministers/priests represent Christ, and he was a man.

Most people would disagree with the first three reasons, today. These old ideas are seen as being **sexist**. The last reason is still believed by a number of Christians, and it is the main reason why the Orthodox and Roman Catholic Churches do not ordain women as priests. They see the priest at the altar as representing Christ in a special way. Others, have different ideas, though.

▲ *Dawn French as the Vicar of Dibley: the parish was surprised to find their new vicar was a woman*

The Reverend Ros Parrett is a priest in Berkshire, running a parish that has a modern building and is among new housing developments.

> ● I was ordained deacon in 1987 and priest In 1994. I took charge of a parish for the first time in 1994 as a team minister. Since 1996 I have been the vicar of a suburban parish.
>
> Yes. I have experienced **prejudice**, but I have also received a great deal of support and prayer from all sorts of people.

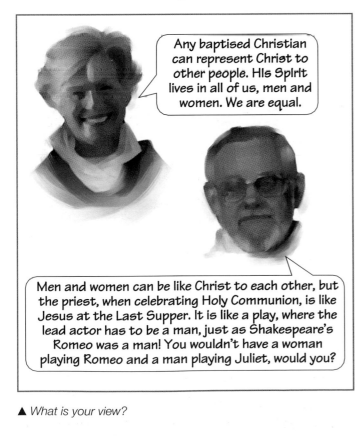

> Any baptised Christian can represent Christ to other people. His Spirit lives in all of us, men and women. We are equal.

> Men and women can be like Christ to each other, but the priest, when celebrating Holy Communion, is like Jesus at the Last Supper. It is like a play, where the lead actor has to be a man, just as Shakespeare's Romeo was a man! You wouldn't have a woman playing Romeo and a man playing Juliet, would you?

▲ *What is your view?*

1 Look at the picture strip on page 38.
   a) Which events are the same each day?
   b) Why do you think the priest goes regularly to church for silent prayer?
   c) He saw some people on their own during these two days. Write down why each one wanted to see the priest.
   d) How do you think the visits would have helped them?

2 **a)** Which reason for not allowing women to be priests still makes sense to some people today?
   b) Why do others argue that women *can* be priests?
   c) What difficulties has the Reverend Ros Parrett faced as a woman priest?
   d) Do you think women should be priests?

3 Invite a Christian minister to talk to your class about the most important aspects of his or her ministry.

4 Are there any aspects of a Christian minister's work which you would like to do? Are there other aspects which you would not like to do? Explain your answers.

◀ *For some, rock climbing is a good way to relax*

Human beings need to play. Too much work makes us dull and stressed. We need times of rest and recreation, to enjoy a sport, go walking, take up a hobby, or read a good book. People now have weekends free, or days off during the week, as well as a few weeks of holiday a year. This was not always the case. In ancient times, the only days off were literally 'holy days', religious festivals. Moses gave the Jews a religious festival each Saturday, one day off every week.

Every major religion has its holy day. The Jews keep Saturday as a day of rest. Jesus himself treated Saturday as the **Sabbath**. In the years after he died, his followers also met on Sundays. This was the day that Jesus had risen from the dead. Naturally, Christians wanted to celebrate this.

But many new followers were not Jewish; they had no reason to treat Saturday as special. So Sunday became the day which Christians used for rest and worship.

However, in many ways, it is like the Jewish Sabbath. It is a day for rest and worship. That is why Sunday is the main day for holding church services in Britain.

There was a time when Christians were very strict about what could not be done on Sundays. In the seventeenth century, you could be fined 50p for selling goods or singing on Sundays.

Until recently, pubs had restricted opening hours on Sunday, most shops could not open, and sports could not be played. Now, all this has changed.

Most Christians want Sunday to be special, but they can still relax, play sport and enjoy themselves, as well as going to Church once or twice a day. Jesus, after all, told people off for being too strict on the Sabbath.

> ● The Sabbath was made for humankind, and not humankind for the Sabbath.
>
> *Mark 2: 27*

But some Christians disagree with this. They think people need a day to rest and refresh themselves for the coming week. They believe Sunday should still be a day for worshipping God. They will not sleep, buy or sell, go to the cinema or play sport.

● I served in the Royal Air Force for two years and was sent off to the north of England. The first Sunday that I was permitted to leave camp I set off to find a church, and got back to camp late that night. And then the questions began.

Where had I been all day? 'I went to church.' That was clear enough, but where did I have my dinner? 'Oh, some people at the church took me home with them to dinner.'

Did I know them before? 'No, I'd never set eyes on them previously.' Well, what about tea? 'I had tea with another family . . . and supper with another family . . . No, I didn't know them either.'

The other men were frankly bewildered. They simply had no experience of a family like that . . . the family of the church.

Peter Cotterell: *This is Christianity*

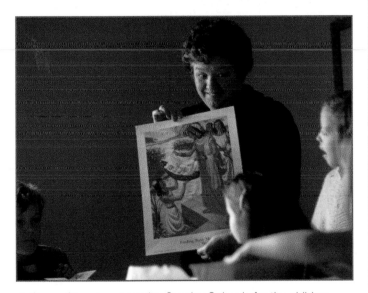
▲ *Some Churches organise Sunday Schools for the children*

We asked some Christians how they tried to make Sunday special. Here are three of their answers.

● **Sandy:** Whenever possible, I always go to church on Sundays, or attend the first mass of Sunday held on Saturday evening. Sundays are my days off. No work or housework. It is a day to be with my husband; a day for doing activities together. It is special because it is the only day when it is possible to spend leisure time together. It is not a 'religious' day as my husband is not a Catholic, but it has a certain Christian spirit.

● **Lynne:** My mum has always attended church and always took me along. Even during my 'rebellion' time which most teenagers go through, my dad forced me to go to church (although he is not a churchgoer).

Therefore, Sunday has been the day when all other plans must fit around church. I have always found it easier to work on a Sunday than on a Saturday. So, in that respect, it's not exactly a 'day of rest'. For years, I have taught Sunday School and, more recently, have also helped at a hospital chapel. So, in some ways, Sunday is also a day of service.

● **Alison:** We always go to church in the morning. We usually have a couple of the single young people from church to Sunday lunch. That's partly because when I was a young student in London I used to go most Sundays to a family and that meant so much to me. So we always have a couple of extra people.

41

1 a) Design a poster, or a collage, of the things you enjoy doing to rest.
b) Write a few lines saying what your favourite leisure activity is, and why.
2 a) List the reasons for having Sunday as a day of rest.
b) What are (i) the advantages and (ii) the disadvantages of shops opening on Sundays?
3 a) Read the passage by Peter Cotterell. Do you think the people who gave him meals were good Christians? Give reasons.

b) Why do you think his friends in the RAF were 'bewildered'?
4 a) Read this page. For each person, write down what she does to make Sunday special.
b) Give reasons why God might be pleased with each person.
c) Is Sunday special for you? If so, explain how it is. If not, suggest at least two ways in which you could make it special.

All Christian Churches have services at which couples get married. Today, people do not have to get married in a church. They can go to a registry office, or another venue, for example a luxury hotel or a paradise island. But about half the Christian marriages in Britain still take place in church.

Marriage services are, of course, happy events. Christians believe that God is present during the service. In front of him, two people are promising to live together as partners until they die. Suppose they were called James and Sarah. These are the **vows** that James would make in an Anglican church. (Sarah would make the same promises.)

*The **vicar** would ask:*

> • James, will you take Sarah to be your wife? Will you love her, comfort her, honour and protect her, and, **forsaking** all others, be faithful to her as long as you both shall live?

James would say:

> • I will.

Soon afterwards, the vicar would place Sarah's right hand in James's right hand and James would repeat these words:

> • I, James, take you, Sarah, to be my wife, to have and to hold from this day forward; for better, for worse, for richer, for poorer, in sickness and in health, to love and to cherish, till death us do part, according to God's holy law; and this is my solemn vow.

The couple also promise to love each other; the woman's wedding ring is a symbol of this. Sometimes, both the bride and the groom give each other a ring. The ring is a symbol of unending love, for it is a circle that goes round and round for ever.

Christians believe that God blesses the marriage – and any children which the couple may have. It is God who has joined the couple together. So some Christian Churches do not approve of divorce.

Roman Catholics, for instance, are not expected to get divorced. If they do, neither husband nor wife can get married in church again. Next time, they would have to use a different venue, such as a registry office. Many Protestant Churches are not always so strict; some will allow divorced people to remarry in church.

Orthodox Christians are allowed to divorce and remarry as it is felt that a relationship can die. The service is shorter, and begins with prayers of forgiveness, the second time around, though. The Church of England blesses couples in church after a second marriage in a registry office.

▲ The bride and groom have just made their vows and the priest declares them to be husband and wife

Here are some things that people say about marriage and families.

A Protestant said:

> ● Give us strong, happy, disciplined families, and we shall be well on the way to a strong nation. So many young people who get into trouble with the law come from broken homes. The family matters, and it's worth working hard to build it, protect it and provide for it.

The Archbishop of Canterbury at the royal wedding in 1981 said:

> ● If we solved all our economic problems and failed to build loving families it would profit us nothing. The family is the place where the future is created good and full of love – or **deformed**.

A Baptist said:

> ● In a marriage ceremony, you become one flesh, with God as head. God is head of our marriage. As we grow together, we should become closer to each other. In so doing, we become closer to God.

▲ *A Russian Orthodox wedding service. Notice the crowns worn by the bride and groom*

A Catholic said:

> ● I would not have felt married in the eyes of the Church if I had been married elsewhere. My faith is important to me so I would not have felt at ease within my marriage unless it had the blessing of the church.

Sadly, marriages can go wrong, though they are intended to be for life. The royal wedding of Prince Charles and Lady Diana was like a fairy tale wedding, but it did not work out. Christians, for all their strong beliefs and hopes, might find that they fail each other. Perhaps the two people develop in very different ways, and they realise that they did not really know what they were doing when they married. Perhaps one has been hard to live with, and has been cruel. Perhaps one partner has been unfaithful. Divorced people then need love and support to build new lives.

43

1 Copy out and complete this paragraph:
   When two Christians get married, the woman is called the _____ and the man is called the _____. During the service, each makes two _____. The bridegroom puts a _____ on the bride's finger, as a symbol of _____.

2 Read the vows that James and Sarah make.
   a) List the five things James promises in the first vow.
   b) In your own words, write down what each one means.
   c) What does he promise in the second vow?
   d) Why do you think he wants to make this promise?

3 Three symbols are mentioned on these pages (see captions as well as main text). Write down each one. Then explain why each is a good symbol.

4 Read the column on the left about marriage.
   a) Why did the Archbishop say families are important?
   b) Do you think people should be allowed to divorce and remarry in church?
   c) Some people who get married in church do not go to church regularly. Do you think they should be made to get married somewhere else? Again, give reasons.

5 Do you want to get married? Explain why or why not.

Each Sunday, Christians remember that Jesus died, yet came back to life. Once a year, there is a special **festival** to remember this. This is called Easter, in English-speaking countries, and a special week builds up to Easter Day, called Holy Week. This recalls the events of the last week in Jesus' life.

◀ *'The Triumphal Entry' – Jesus rides into Jerusalem*

● Holy Week

● PALM SUNDAY

Holy Week begins on Palm Sunday. This remembers the time when Jesus entered Jerusalem riding on a donkey. The crowds waved palm branches before him. This custom meant that Jesus was being honoured as the coming king. He had chosen to enter this way to fulfil a prophecy in the Hebrew Scriptures, 'Lo, your king comes to you; triumphant and victorious is he, humble and riding on a donkey . . .' (Zechariah 9: 9)

● MONDAY–WEDNESDAY

Jesus taught the people in Jerusalem, as the leaders began to plot against him.

● MAUNDY THURSDAY

Jesus held the Last Supper with the disciples. He washed their feet to make the point that he had come to help and serve them. (Foot washing was the action of a servant, usually. This was a common custom in a hot, sandy country.)

▲ *Jesus washes the disciples' feet at the Last Supper*

Later that evening, Jesus went outside the city into the Garden of Gethsemane to pray with his disciples. He knew he was about to be arrested, praying, 'Abba, Father, for you all things are possible; remove this cup from me; yet not what I want, but what you want.' Then, soldiers came to arrest him and the disciples fled.

● GOOD FRIDAY

▲ *Jesus, crucified with two thieves*

Jesus was sentenced to death and nailed to a cross. The Romans executed thieves and criminals in this way. They probably thought that Jesus was a troublemaker who wanted the people to rebel against them. The women disciples stayed with Jesus, and one other, unnamed man. Two thieves were crucified with him. One cursed Jesus, one asked for help. Jesus promised him that he would be with him in Paradise that very day. By the afternoon, Jesus was dead.

● HOLY SATURDAY

▲ *The garden tomb, sealed by a large heavy stone*

Jesus was buried in someone else's tomb, which he had donated. It was cut into the rock, with a huge stone rolled over the entrance.

● EASTER SUNDAY

Early in the morning, some of the women disciples came to the tomb to ask permission to wash and prepare the body according to Jewish custom, out of respect. Jesus had been buried in a hurry, as the Sabbath was approaching, and no work could be done. They found the tomb empty, with the stone rolled back. The graveclothes were lying where the body had been left. Visions followed, as the risen Jesus appeared to them and to the men, in Galilee and in Jerusalem.

▲ *The risen Christ, blazing with holy light*

The disciples stopped hiding and were filled with courage to carry on Jesus' work. They believed that Jesus was alive in a new, spiritual way. He had been glorified and taken into heaven.

1 Draw a series of six Easter Eggs, one for each of the times or days described on these pages. Label these, and write a sentence in each one saying what happened to Jesus. Also, draw a scene, or a symbol, in each one. Use two pages of your exercise books, or a sheet of plain paper.

2 Watch the events of Holy Week on a video film of the life of Jesus, such as 'Jesus of Nazareth'.

3 The empty cross is a Christian symbol of hope. Light and spring are universal symbols of hope. What other symbols of hope can you think of? Design your own badge with a symbol of hope on it.

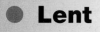

Lent

Christians prepare for Easter for a period of forty days, called Lent. This begins on Ash Wednesday, and many Churches have the custom of putting ashes on a person's forehead. Ashes are a symbol of sorrow for sin, and a reminder that we are from the earth, mortal. The priest says either, 'Turn away from sin and be faithful to the gospel' or 'Remember that you are dust, and to dust you will return.'

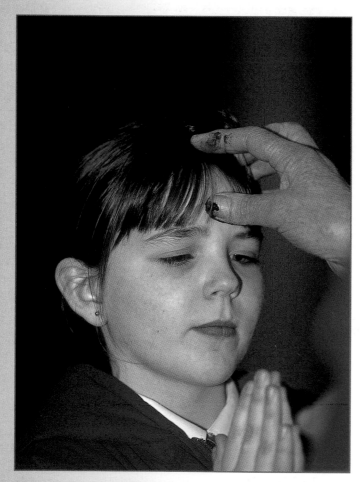

▲ A child receives ashes on her forehead on Ash Wednesday

Christians make an extra effort in Lent. Some spend more time praying, or thinking of kind things to do. Some study the Bible together, or give something up, like chocolate.

Holy Week is celebrated by re-enacting aspects of Jesus' life.

● PALM SUNDAY

Palm crosses or branches are carried around the Church in procession, recalling the entry of Jesus into Jerusalem.

Some Churches also have a donkey to lead the procession.

▲ Preparing for Palm Sunday procession. Why do you think a donkey leads this?

● MONDAY–WEDNESDAY

There will be an extra communion service in the evening, or a time for prayer. Some Churches hold 'the Stations of the Cross', where people pray in front of pictures of Jesus on his journey to the cross.

● MAUNDY THURSDAY

The word 'Maundy' comes from the Latin *mandatum* meaning 'commandment'. This refers to the new commandment that Jesus gave to love one another. He demonstrated this by washing his disciples' feet, and many churches repeat this action as part of the service. Special thanksgivings are said for the gift of Holy Communion, too, and people pray silently after the service at a side altar where flowers are arranged, representing the Garden of Gethsemane.

46

● GOOD FRIDAY

▲ *A family prays before a cross on Good Friday*

On Good Friday Christians remember the death of Jesus. Many churches remove all decorations so that they are plain and bare. The story of the Passion (Jesus suffering on the cross) is read out, and a cross might be used as a focal point. Some people **venerate** this, touching, kissing or bowing low before it. When this is brought into the Church, the priest will say, 'This is the wood of the cross on which hung the Saviour of the world.'

This is '*Good* Friday' as Jesus died to save people and forgive their sins.

● EASTER EVE

Easter Eve comes at the end of Holy Saturday. No services are held during Holy Saturday to recall Jesus lying in the tomb. The first service of Easter is in the evening, after sunset. This celebrates the resurrection. A bonfire blazes, symbolising the light and new life of Christ, and the paschal candle is lit from this. This is carried into the Church as the priest says, 'The light of Christ' and all the people light smaller candles from this, passing a wave of light around the place in minutes.

▲ *Lighting the paschal candle on Easter Eve*

● EASTER SUNDAY

Morning services celebrate the resurrection, and it is a time of great joy. The Church is full of flowers and decorations.

Easter uses the themes of darkness and light. Human life is full of hard times and suffering, but also hopes and joys. Joy came after tears, light from darkness. Jesus died but rose again.

---

1 What do Christians do on each of these days, and why? Palm Sunday; Maundy Thursday; Good Friday; Easter Eve; Easter Sunday.
2 Holy Week uses symbols. Can you find out what these are?
3 Easter is about darkness turning into light. Can you think of a time when life was difficult for you, and then things turned out better than you hoped for? If not, make up a story where this happens to someone.

● Christmas

Easter is the most important Christian festival, but Christmas is the most popular. The Bible does not say when Jesus was born. So the Romans picked 25 December as the day for the celebrations. It was already part of a Roman festival for the sun god.

Today, Christians get ready for Christmas four Sundays beforehand. The period leading up to Christmas is known as Advent. Some churches put out an Advent **wreath**, with five candles. Each Sunday, a new one is lit.

Finally, on Christmas Day itself, they light the fifth candle. Remember that light is an important Christian symbol. For Christians, Jesus is *the Light of the World*.

Orthodox Christians in Britain also remember the day with special events.

Twelve days after Christmas is the feast of the Epiphany. This remembers the visit of the shepherds and the wise men from the East. It was the day when Jesus was 'shown' to the world. Eastern Orthodox Christians still celebrate Christmas at this time.

Christians also remember the saints of the Church, outstanding holy men and women who set an example. December 6th is the feast day of St Nicholas, the Bishop of Myra, in Turkey. The legend of Santa Claus, or Father Christmas, is based upon this real man who lived in the fourth century CE. One of his good deeds involved throwing three golden balls down a chimney to pay for three girls to get married, so they would not be sold into slavery.

▲ *A girl lights the fifth candle on the Advent wreath on Christmas Day*

▲ *Saint Nicholas*

Saints are painted in Orthodox icons as having light shining from their faces, for they are full of the glory of God.

◄ *A Baptist Pentecost banner*

Harvest

In autumn, Harvest festivals are held. Church members bring gifts of food to the service, and these are distributed afterwards to the elderly and needy in the area. A large harvest loaf, baked in the style of wheat sheaves, will usually be placed near the altar. Christians give thanks to God the creator for the earth, and nature. Many charities are supported with harvest gifts, and some people collect money for environmental action groups, such as 'Friends of the Earth', or particular causes such as the Scottish based 'Trees for Life'. This group is trying to replant the Caledonian forest in the Highlands of Scotland. Only 1% of the original forest land still survives. Much of the wildlife has died out, too.

Pentecost

Another major Christian festival is Pentecost. This remembers the gift of the Holy Spirit to the first disciples. Acts 2: 1–11 tells this story, using the symbols of wind and fire to describe the Spirit. Wind is powerful, and cannot be seen, and fire burns up rubbish and gives light.

Christians used to baptise new believers on the Day of Pentecost, and the women wore white dresses. For this reason, the festival was known as White Sunday (Whitsun, for short). 'Walks of witness' were held through the towns, with people carrying banners and singing songs. These customs are not so common today.

▲ *Replanted trees in the Caledonian forest*

---

1 a) What events do these festivals remind Christians of: (i) Christmas; (ii) Pentecost; (iii) Harvest.

b) Explain the meaning of (i) Advent; (ii) Epiphany; (iii) Whitsun.

2 a) What do the symbols of wind and fire suggest about the Holy Spirit?

b) Talk about a time when you have been trying to walk in the wind, or sail in difficult conditions.

c) Talk about a time when you have found sitting around a fire comforting, or a time when fire was scary.

3 How do you think the Father Christmas legend developed from St Nicholas and the three golden balls? Draw a cartoon of St Nicholas throwing the gold into the house.

4 Think up your own festival to celebrate one of these events: (i) the end of a war; (ii) a thanksgiving for coal, oil and gas; (iii) a thanksgiving for air. Describe where it would happen, and choose some good symbols for the service. You could draw these.

5 Write to 'Trees for Life' at The Park, Findhorn Bay, Forres IV36 0TZ, Scotland, or 'Friends of the Earth', 26–28 Underwood Street, London N1 7JQ, or another charity of your choice. Find out more information about their work, and see if your class could do something to support them.

Life is like a journey from birth to death. We move through life, and go through many experiences. A person with faith in God is on a journey of faith, learning new things about themselves and about God. To help think about this journey, many Christians go on a **pilgrimage**, a journey to a special place. Once there, they seek answers, or spend time in prayer, and return to their normal life refreshed.

Some of the main places of pilgrimage are marked on the map. Places become special either because they are associated with events in the life of Jesus or a saint, or the Virgin Mary is said to have appeared there.

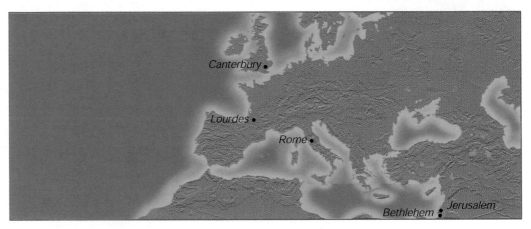

► Some of the main places of pilgrimage for Christians

● Bethlehem

▲ Inside the Church of the Nativity. The star marks the spot where people think Jesus was born

The Church of the Nativity is built over the traditional site of the birth of Jesus. A star design shows the spot where people think this happened.

● Jerusalem

Jerusalem is a holy city for Jews, Christians and Muslims. This is where Jesus was crucified and buried. The Church of the Holy Sepulchre stands over the traditional site of the tomb of Jesus. Only part of the original tomb exists, the burial slab shown here.

▲ The old, stone slab is all that remains of an ancient tomb. Many Christians believe that this was the tomb of Jesus. This is inside the Church of the Holy Sepulchre

● Rome

▲ *Pope John Paul II, head of the Roman Catholic Church*

Rome is important for many Christians because this is where the Pope, the head of the Roman Catholic church, lives. Roman Catholics believe he is the successor to St Peter, and Peter is believed to be buried beneath St Peter's Church.

● Lourdes

▲ *Pilgrims visit Lourdes hoping to be healed*

The shrine of Our Lady of Lourdes, in France, began in the nineteenth century CE. A young peasant girl, Bernadette, saw a vision of Mary in 1858, by the rose bush at the entrance to a grotto. This happened several times, and eventually Bernadette was told that a spring would appear, and that people were to come to be healed. A church has been built over the grotto and spring, and thousands of visitors come each year.

Why do Christians go on pilgrimage? They might want to:
● say sorry for something they have done wrong and ask for forgiveness
● gain strength to face the future
● ask for help for someone else
● feel at peace
● show their faith in God.

1 Match up the places on the left with the descriptions on the right.

Rome	the place where Jesus was born
Jerusalem	where the Virgin Mary appeared to St Bernadette
Lourdes	where Jesus was crucified and buried
Bethlehem	where the Pope lives and St Peter is believed to be buried.

2 a) Look at the reasons for going on a pilgrimage. Write down a reason why you might go on a pilgrimage. Give reasons for your choice.

b) Compare your class's results. Work out the top choice and discuss your different reasons.

3 a) In what ways is life like a journey? Discuss this in groups.

b) Draw a pathway. Draw, or write along this, marking on important things that have happened to you in your life so far.

There are important places of pilgrimage in Britain, too.

Canterbury

▲ *The Archbishop of Canterbury, George Carey (centre)*

Canterbury is the cathedral of the Archbishop of Canterbury, the senior bishop in the Church of England. The Cathedral contains the tomb of a saint from the Middle Ages, St Thomas a Becket. He was Archbishop when Henry II was king, and he was murdered in the Cathedral on 29 December 1170. He was known as a kind and saintly bishop. He was soon declared to be a saint, and many people believed that his prayers had helped them. The writer, Chaucer, based his *Canterbury Tales* upon a group of pilgrims travelling there. The shrine was destroyed by Henry VIII when he separated from the Pope, but many pilgrims continued to visit the site where it stood.

Walsingham

Walsingham is a small village in Norfolk. The Lady Richeldis had a vision of Mary in 1061. She was told to build a copy of the house where Jesus was brought up in Nazareth. People were to come here to seek healing and peace. A spring appeared, and monks ran a monastery and a shrine Church built around the Holy House. It was very popular, and people travelled from all over Europe. There were many stories of miracles.

In the sixteenth century the old shrine was destroyed by Henry VIII, who wanted its riches. It lay in ruins until early in the twentieth century when the vicar of the Anglican parish, Alfred Hope Patten, raised the funds to rebuild it. Today, there is a shrine Church and a new Holy House inside, with many buildings where pilgrims can stay.

▶ *Inside the Anglican shrine of Our Lady of Walsingham*

● Miracles on Pilgrimage?

Many sick people claim they were cured after going to Lourdes. The Catholic Church says that, up to 1979, only 65 of these were **miracles**.

Before deciding if a cure was a miracle, it asks these questions:

● Was the disease serious?
● Was the cure sudden and unexpected?
● Was it a complete cure?
● Did it last at least three years?
● Was it proved by tests, X-rays, etc?
● Did any medical treatment help the cure?

Edeltraud Fulda had suffered from a serious illness for thirteen years before going to Lourdes in 1950. After bathing at Lourdes, she felt cured. Doctors confirmed this and the Church accepted it as a miracle.

Before

After

▲ *Edeltraud Fulda was cured after visiting Lourdes*

Andrea Jackson was badly injured when she was eight. She was taken to hospital in a critical condition. Her parents tell the story:

> ● They told us that Andrea wasn't expected to live the night. She had major surgery where they'd removed the biggest part of the left-hand side of her skull.
>
> After we'd had a discussion with the surgeon, we told him that, if Andrea had to live by machine, it wanted turning off. We wouldn't allow her to be kept on the machine. After they brought Andrea out of surgery, we were prepared for the worst.

Then, at the Anglican shrine at Walsingham in Norfolk, another girl was anointed at the Holy Well. Meanwhile, holy water was sprinkled on Andrea herself in hospital. Andrea had known nothing about the shrine. This was what happened next:

> ● They brought her round. When they took the tubes out of her nose and throat, she just looked around and said, 'I've been to Walsingham.'
>
> We stood back in amazement. She'd been unconscious for most of a week. We couldn't understand why she should say such a thing.
>
> We feel we owe Walsingham something. We believe that Andrea was made better through the prayers of our Lady of Walsingham.
>
> BBC Television: *England's Nazareth*

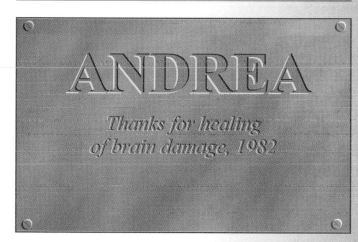

▲ *The thanksgiving plaque made after Andrea's healing*

1 a) What is a miracle?

b) Explain how the Roman Catholic Church lays down strict rules to decide if a miracle happens. How many miracles have they recognised at Lourdes between 1858 and 1979?

c) Read what happened to Andrea Jackson. What do you find most surprising about these events? Give reasons for your choices.

d) Do you think the girl's recovery was a miracle? Give reasons.

e) Imagine you were one of her parents. Write two diary entries. The first describes your feelings after talking to the surgeon; the second gives your feelings when she comes round.

2 Design your own banner to carry on a pilgrimage. Then, explain how you chose your design.

The 'Star Trek' series has a mission for its crew, 'to boldly go where no man has gone before', exploring the universe. They seek out new civilisations and intelligent races to learn new ideas and share knowledge with them. A mission is a task that you are sent on, a challenge. It is not necessarily something religious.

Jesus himself asked his followers to go out and teach about him. Some of the early Christians travelled around the Roman Empire, spreading the good news about Jesus. Christian monks brought the Gospel to Britain in the first few centuries after Jesus died.

A **missionary** is a person who travels to teach about Jesus – a missionary can be a man or a woman, a lay person or a priest, a monk or a nun. There are still missionary organisations which train and sponsor missionaries to go out to different parts of the world.

▲ Protestors with a mission

Some people are on a mission to save the environment. These 'Greenpeace' demonstrators are campaigning against nuclear power stations.

YES!
missionaries still exist.
NO!
missionaries are not out of date.

Missionaries? Missions? The name doesn't matter, but . . .

Middle East Christian Outreach

is glad to be a fellowship of those who believe in reaching out in the love of Jesus Christ to lost men and women.

Middle East Christian Outreach

needs missionaries - or whatever you like to call people who are willing to move with God, wherever, however and whenever he directs.

WHAT KIND OF PEOPLE ARE NEEDED?

▲ Part of a pamphlet from Middle East Christian Outreach (MECO)

▲ A missionary's jobs

Being a missionary today involves more than teaching and preaching. It often involves practical help, and missionaries need medical skills or farming skills to help local communities. The message of Jesus is not just about going to heaven and being forgiven, but loving one another now. Love in action means help where it is needed.

Bishop Allison was a missionary in the Sudan.

● I was asked by some schoolboys at our junior secondary school why I had come to the Sudan at all. I could only say something like this, 'because I believe somehow that God has called me. Don't ask me to explain how. Others have influenced me and played a part. And, I think, because I felt it offered adventure in the service of Jesus Christ.'

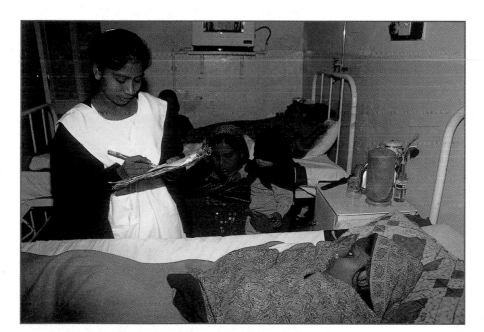

◄ A Christian Mission hospital in Pakistan

1 In groups, think up a worthwhile mission for today's world. It might be saving the rainforest. Design an advert, asking for people with certain skills to help with this mission. What practical skills would you need? What communication skills? What media or musical skills?

2 Define what a Christian missionary is.

3 Look at the cartoon on this page. Which of the missionary's jobs do you think is the most important? Can you think of any other things they might need to do?

4 a) Look at the message from MECO. What type of person do you think they are looking for? Choose four of the following words that would best describe a good missionary and explain why.
(i) happy; (ii) hard-working; (iii) lazy; (iv) Christian; (v) energetic; (vi) weak; (vii) brave; (viii) good; (ix) loving; (x) athletic; (xi) caring; (xii) bad-tempered; (xiii) healthy.

b) Imagine you were a missionary today. You have just arrived in a new country where you don't know anybody. Make a list of the things you need to do in the first few days.

c) Make up an advert, asking for people to become missionaries in another country. Make it as appealing as you can.

Soap operas are popular. They are an escape and entertainment. We follow the stories and get hooked. They reflect issues in modern life, but they are also artificial, contrived. They work to set formulas:

- relationship problems
- family break-ups or get-togethers
- sudden tragedies (illness, car crash).

Yet, soaps usually suggest that what people really bother about today is getting their own way, finding out what they really want. If other people get hurt in the process, then that's sad, but that's life. A wife leaves her family to find a new start, a boy goes out with someone else because it feels good. *Putting yourself first*, finding your *own* fulfilment, is a very modern message.

▲ *Is this your idea of a committed Christian?*

In complete contrast, many people think Christians are not bothered about themselves at all – or they should not be. A committed Christian is seen as a monk type, who has few possessions and gives all his or her money away. Priests are often asked by young people, 'Do you get paid?' or 'Do you live in a Church?' or even, 'Do you eat?' as though they are ghostly figures, unreal and heavenly.

What we see in these two extremes – putting yourself first, and putting everyone else first – is a lack of balance. As human beings, Christians or not, we need to look after ourselves, and to remember that we are part of society. We need to help and to be helped by others. We also need our own space and pleasure.

Jesus taught people, 'Love your neighbour as yourself.' This is a perfect balance, for he did not ask people to love others and forget about themselves. If you can't love yourself, you are not much good to anyone else. Pope John Paul II has also said: 'Human beings are not made to live alone. They are born into a family and in a family they grow, eventually entering society through their activity.' Or, as a poet said, 'No man is an island.'

Relationships depend upon trust, especially romantic ones. When a boy and girl go out with each other, they open themselves to one another. Think of how defences come down, and you stop pretending to be someone you are not. You are real, yourself, and you let your partner see your weaknesses. Relationships break down when that trust is broken, when secrets are not kept, or you make fun of your friend. Not respecting their wishes leads to the end of the relationship. Some people feel they *need* a relationship, and seek to control and dominate their partner. That is a road to nowhere.

● Sex?

Sexual relationships are not just like kissing and holding hands. Sex involves deep feelings and a bond between people. The Bible writers had a phrase for having sex, 'to *know* someone'. If we trivialise this, and have sex too easily and freely, it loses its dignity and people open themselves up to being hurt – not only with the risk of unwanted pregnancy or sexually transmitted diseases, but also in their emotions. A girl might give up her virginity out of love, only to find that the boy moves on, and she is 'dumped'. The rejection goes deep. Pressure can be put on the partner to have sex when he or she is not ready.

True love does not force someone else. Remember the words of St Paul: 'Love is patient; love is kind . . . It does not insist on its own way.'

The Church has always wanted to put a protective fence around sex, as it is something so special, precious and delicate. Most Christians say that this should be only within marriage, where a formal, legal commitment has been made between two people to build their lives together. There is a lively debate today, though, as society has changed so much. A number of people choose to live together. Is their wanting to be together a sign of their commitment, and as good as a marriage? Perhaps sex belongs in a *committed relationship*, though there might be many different forms of that.

'If you love me you will . . .'

▲ *Under pressure . . .*

▶ *An Eastern image of Jesus, showing him as he would have been – black haired and dark skinned*

Soap operas often deal with racism. Many areas of Britain have people of different races living together. Racism is prejudice against someone because of their race. Many things can cause it:

- fear of people who look or act different
- fear of losing jobs to people who are from other countries
- being too proud of our own customs and feeling superior
- lies and half-truths about the way of life of others.

One older white couple were racist about Asians. Their teenage son's best friend happened to be Asian. He was afraid to bring the boy home. When he did, his parents were on their best behaviour. Afterwards, their son said, 'You were so nice to him . . . but I thought you didn't like Asians!' 'Oh, he's all right . . .' they said, 'it's all the others we don't like!' This story shows how people fear what they do not know and understand. In meeting the Asian youth, they met a fellow human being, whom they could not help liking.

Christianity teaches that there is one God who made all people, of many different races and customs. No one race is better than any others – black, white, Chinese and Asian, for example, are all equal. We are part of one world. Jesus would have been coloured, as he came from the Middle East, and he would have looked like an Arab.

Christians are not all white people from Europe. Any race or nationality can be a Christian believer – there are African, Indian and Chinese Churches, for example. St Paul said, 'There is no longer Jew nor Greek, there is no longer slave or free, there is no longer male and female; for you are all one in Christ Jesus.'

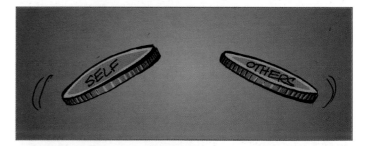

1 **a)** In the 'Others' side of the coin, draw and write about some people who mean a great deal to you.
   b) In the 'Self' side, draw or write about something you are pleased with about yourself – a skill, a hobby, a pet, a possession.
   c) Write out Jesus' commandment about love.

2 Talk, as a class, about some soap operas that you are watching, and the issues that arise from them.

3 In groups, make lists of all the ingredients you need to have a successful relationship with someone.

4 Write a letter to a Problem Page from a girl who is worried that her boyfriend is putting her under pressure to have sex with him. Then write the reply.

5 Design a leaflet, 'Beware of Racism!'. List the reasons why some people are racist, and say why they should not be.

6 Imagine that you are a vicar on a TV discussion. You are asked, 'Why does Christianity say that racism is wrong?' What would you say?

- I will show you my faith by my actions.

  James 2: 18

- I give you a new commandment that you love one another.

  Jesus, in John 13: 24

The world changes all the time, and there are new problems to face. Christian beliefs are the same though, and Christians feel challenged to show the same care and love for others that Jesus showed. This means accepting people whom others might find it hard to accept. It means being available, and listening when someone wants to talk. It means being open, and not rejecting someone who has not had such a fortunate life.

Of course, sometimes Christians are faced with hard decisions, just like anyone else. After all, many modern problems did not exist in Jesus' time.

▲ *Some schools, like the one shown above, provide lessons on drugs education – just one of today's problems that did not exist when Jesus was alive*

But, above all, they believe that Jesus loves them. Like Mother Teresa, they try to show the same love and care for others, especially those who are less lucky than they are. They try to teach people to love one another.

In this chapter we look at what two organisations are doing to improve our world. We do not show everything which Christians are doing – that would be impossible! However, this gives an idea of the range of things which Christians do in their efforts to follow Jesus.

This is what the Salvation Army says about itself and its work.

- . . . a worldwide Christian Movement whose members are happy, sincere followers of Jesus Christ. They try to serve Him by helping needy people in the best possible way.

  Members of the Army are called Salvationists. They are involved in many kinds of activities:
  - preaching the gospel
  - running playgroups
  - playing in bands
  - treating sickness
  - praising God
  - praying
  - studying the Bible
  - feeding the hungry
  - caring for the homeless

  All of these activities have the same purpose – to make the world a happy place, for God's sake.

- The little blue van heads towards the midnight haunts of the homeless who sleep rough. The first stop is just off fashionable Oxford Street. There is nobody to be seen. But suddenly the piles of cardboard by the wall begin to move and fall away – men are sleeping in and under the cardboard boxes.

  Soon some twenty men are waiting for supper. Everybody knows the Captain and his team. The approach is casual. There is no preaching. The men are almost unaware that they are being treated kindly, feeling warmed and cheered as they drink the soup and eat the bread.

  It is simply taken from the wrapper and handed out. But an observer said it was like celebrating Communion, as he sensed the presence of Christ.

Christian **Aid**
We believe in life before death

Christian Aid is an organisation which helps people in developing countries to build better lives.

● Friada Nordez works in rice fields in Mozambique. She has to use a large snail shell to cut the crop as she has no sickle (no tools). Imagine how long it takes!

   The nearest market is fifteen miles away and the roads are poor. To stop the women from having to carry heavy loads, Christian Aid supports a farmers' association which buys their harvest and takes it to market by tractor.

▲ Cutting crops with a shell is hard work

• Christian Aid supports a vaccination programme in schools in Haiti to help stop diseases spreading.

▲ These school girls are being vaccinated to stop the spread of disease

1 Make a collection of materials which show what Christians are doing in the world today. You could use your school library or visit your local church(es). You could also write to organisations such as the Salvation Army. Their addresses are on the right. (Please remember to send postage.) When you have collected these items, you could make a collage for your classroom. Each member of your group could write about one item and add the writing to the collage.
2 In groups, discuss what you think are the most serious problems facing the world today. When you have chosen five, discuss whether you think they will change as you get older. What do you think the most serious problems will be by the year 2010?
3 Draw an outline of the snail shell and write a thank you message inside this to Christian Aid, from Friada.

Useful Addresses

● The Salvation Army, 101 Queen Victoria Street, London EC4P 4EP
● Christian Aid, PO Box 100, London SE1 7RT
● Missionaries of Charity, 177 Bravington Road, London W9
● USPG, 157 Waterloo Road, London SE1 8UU
● Middle East Christian Outreach, 22 Culverdon Park Road, Tunbridge Wells, Kent TN4 9RU
● Methodist Church Overseas Division, 25 Marylebone Road, London, NW1 5JR
● Church Missionary Society, 157 Waterloo Road, London SE1 8UU

Glossary

almighty – possessing all power

altar – stand or table in the holiest part of a church

Anglican – member of the Church of England

anointed – put oil on

Apocrypha – books accepted as part of holy scripture by Catholics, but not by Protestants

apostle – one of the twelve men Christ chose to preach the gospel

ascended – went up

authority – power

baptised – dipped into water or having water sprinkled on the head as a sign of washing away sin

Bible study group – group of people who meet to study and discuss the Bible

bishop – clergyman in charge of a diocese (church district)

canon – clergyman attached to a cathedral

catacomb – underground burial place

catholic – including the whole Christian church; worldwide, universal

chaplain – clergyman who works with an organisation, such as a hospital, or a family

chrism – scented olive oil which is blessed by a bishop

chrismation – in the Orthodox Churches, the newly baptised are blessed by applying the oil of chrism as a sign of the gift of the Holy Spirit

commandment – law

conceived – born

confessing – admitting

congregation – people who have come together to worship

conscience – sense of right and wrong

counsellor – person who advises

creator – person who makes something

crucifix – cross with a figure of Christ crucified on it

deformed – made ugly or not normal

disciple – follower of Jesus

divine – of God; holy

ecumenical – 'one world'; the movement to unite all Christians together

epidemic – widespread

eternally – existing for always

extra-sensory knowledge – experiencing or being aware of things beyond our five senses

festival – celebration, often in memory of something

forsaking – giving up

Gospel – teachings of Jesus

governor – man who rules an area

Holy Spirit – the unseen spirit of God

humility – being humble, not thinking too much of ourselves

icon – holy picture of a holy person, such as Christ

inspired – put thought or feeling into

lay – not a clergyman

Lent – forty days before Easter; a time of confessing sins

minister – clergyman serving a church

miracle – event which goes against the laws of nature

missionary – person who travels to spread the Christian faith

non-conformist – Protestant outside the Church of England

obituary – an account of a person's life and their achievements which appears in a newspaper after their death

ordained – appointed as a Christian minister

Orthodox – the word means 'right worship'. Many Eastern Churches are called 'Orthodox Churches'

parable – short story with a meaning

pilgrimage – journey to a holy place

prejudice – being biased about something or someone before you know all the facts

priest – clergyman or minister of a Christian Church

prophecy – a message from God, which might sometimes foretell the future

prophet – a messenger of God

pulpit – platform in a church from which the minister preaches

rector – Anglican clergyman in charge of a parish

redeemed – made up for

renounce – give up

repent – ask forgiveness for sin

resurrection – coming back to life

retreat – time spent at a quiet place of rest

Roman Catholic – the Church which recognises the Pope, in Rome, as their leader

Sabbath – day of rest and worship

saint – very holy person

scripture – holy writing

sermon – public talk about religion

sexist – prejudiced against someone because of their sex

shrine – holy place

slums – crowded, dirty part of town

soul – the person, the self, which Christians believe will survive the death of the body

staid – quiet and steady

venerate – to honour and respect a holy object, such as a cross or an icon. This might involve bowing before it and/or kissing it

vicar – see rector

visions – powerful experiences, like a waking dream, that are seen by some people. They believe God is communicating with them

vow – promise

worshipping – paying honour and respect (to God)

wreath – ring of leaves or flowers twisted together

Index